Ruth: Diamonds in the Darkness

Ruth:
Diamonds in the Darkness

Word of His Mouth Publishers
Mooresboro, NC

All Scripture quotations are taken from the **King James Version** of the Bible.

ISBN: 978-1-941039-03-8
Printed in the United States of America
©2018 Dr. Bo Wagner (Robert Arthur Wagner)

Word of His Mouth Publishers
Mooresboro, NC
www.wordofhismouth.com

Cover art by Chip Nuhrah

Table of Contents

Introduction

There is, I believe, no greater human love story in the history of time or eternity than what we find in the little four-chapter book of Ruth. People who have been saved for a while or been in church for a while have already, no doubt, heard many times about how the love story of Ruth and Boaz is a picture of the love story of Christ and us. And that position is certainly correct. Boaz was Ruth's kinsman redeemer; the Lord Jesus Christ is our Kinsman Redeemer. Boaz took all of the debt of Ruth to himself and gave her all of his riches; Christ took all of our sin debt to Himself and gave us all of His riches.

But that is just one of the many aspects of this book. When I was a young and overly hyper pastor, on two occasions I taught through the book of Ruth in Sunday school, and on both occasions, I did it one chapter per lesson. When I got a little older, though, and learned to slow down for things that deserve slowing down over, it occurred to me just how much of an injustice that really was. This book deserves a far more in-depth hearing than that. There are treasures in this book and lessons in this book that I dare not skim over in such a manner any more.

My third time around through Ruth ended up producing this book. May it be a blessing to you as you read it and think on it.

Chapter 1
From Darkness into Darkness

Ruth 1:1 *Now it came to pass in the days when the judges ruled, that there was a famine in the land. And a certain man of Bethlehemjudah went to sojourn in the country of Moab, he, and his wife, and his two sons.* **2** *And the name of the man was Elimelech, and the name of his wife Naomi, and the name of his two sons Mahlon and Chilion, Ephrathites of Bethlehemjudah. And they came into the country of Moab, and continued there.*

A dark time in God's country

Ruth 1:1a *Now it came to pass in the days when the judges ruled, that there was a famine in the land...*

Please let me take a moment and teach you a little something about your Bible. In your Bible, the tiny little book of Ruth is only four chapters long.

Just to the left of Ruth, though, one page before you get there, you are in the book called Judges. Just to the right of Ruth, one page after you leave there, you are in the book of 1 Samuel. There is maybe 1/1000 of an inch between Judges and 1 Samuel.

But there is a stark difference in the trajectory of these two books. You can think of Judges as a sharp trajectory downward on a graph, and you can think of 1 Samuel as a sharp trajectory upward on a graph.

There is going to be a change in the form of government between the time of the Judges and the time of Samuel. Samuel was a prophet and is also usually regarded as the last of the judges, and he was the man that was going to be used by God to usher in the monarchy in Israel.

Samuel was going to anoint Saul of Benjamin as the first king. But Saul was not even God's preferred choice in that matter. Israel got ahead of God because of all that went on during the period of the judges. The second man that Samuel anointed, David from the tribe of Judah, was God's plan all along. Under David and then his son Solomon, the nation of Israel solidified and became powerful and wealthy. They worshiped, especially under David, the one true God alone. They were led by a man who was strong and sure and was described as "a man after God's own heart."

If Elimelech had lived during the days of the monarchy under David, it is very likely that nothing that you read in the book of Ruth ever would have taken place. He was just a few short generations removed from that time period, but that made all the difference in the land and in this historical account. If you were able to pick up the book of Ruth and move it to the right a bit and put it during the time period of the monarchy under David, the whole story would have changed for the land and for this family.

But Elimelech lived under the judges. That book of Ruth that you are looking at, in your mind you need to pick it up and move it to the left a bit. It did not happen while things were going on that upward trajectory; it happened while things were going on that downward trajectory. It did not happen while there was a single consistent "man after God's own heart" kind of ruler; it happened in a time where there were a whole bunch of different, less consistent, less powerful leaders. It happened at a time when the people of Israel were in constant turmoil and upheaval.

Believe me when I tell you there has never been a darker, more sordid time in all the history of the nation of Israel.

10

And this backdrop is essential to understand when considering the book of Ruth. When you really begin to wrap your mind around just how bad things were, then it makes the famine and the foolish choice of Elimelech make a lot more sense.

The New Testament put a time frame on how long all of this lasted:

Acts 13:20 *And after that he gave unto them judges about the space of four hundred and fifty years, until Samuel the prophet.*

Moses died and then Joshua took over leading the people. From Joshua until the time that Samuel came to prominence, the time of the judges, there were about 450 years. During that 450-year period there was a cycle that repeated itself over and over and over and over and over and again:

Judges 2:13 *And they forsook the LORD, and served Baal and Ashtaroth.* **14** *And the anger of the LORD was hot against Israel, and he delivered them into the hands of spoilers that spoiled them, and he sold them into the hands of their enemies round about, so that they could not any longer stand before their enemies.* **15** *Whithersoever they went out, the hand of the LORD was against them for evil, as the LORD had said, and as the LORD had sworn unto them: and they were greatly distressed.* **16** *Nevertheless the LORD raised up judges, which delivered them out of the hand of those that spoiled them.* **17** *And yet they would not hearken unto their judges, but they went a whoring after other gods, and bowed themselves unto them: they turned quickly out of the way which their fathers walked in, obeying the commandments of the LORD; but they did not so.* **18** *And when the LORD raised them up judges, then the LORD was with the judge, and delivered them out of the hand of their enemies all the days of the judge: for it repented the LORD because of their groanings by reason of them that oppressed them and vexed them.* **19** *And it came to pass, when the judge was dead, that they returned, and corrupted themselves more than their fathers,* *in following other gods to serve them, and to bow down unto them; they ceased not from their own doings, nor from their stubborn way.*

The people would forsake God and follow false gods. God would remove His hand of protection from them and allow a foreign power to overrun them and put them into harsh bondage. Their bondage would wake them up to how sinful they had been and how much they needed God. They would cry out to God for mercy. God would raise up a judge, a deliverer, who would help them to overthrow their enemies. They would follow that judge and do right for a while, but when the judge died, they would go back to the beginning of the cycle again—forsaking God and following after false gods. They did this time after time after time after time. And then when you compound that by the fact that some of their judges were as bad or worse than they were, you will understand why things got bad in Israel.

In Judges 9, a man had seventy of his own family members murdered so he could gain the throne.

In Judges 11, a married man named Gilead had a fling with a prostitute, and a son named Jephthah came from that union. When little Jephthah grew up some, his half-brothers chased him out of the country, then when they needed him to fight for them, they brought him back and "promised to be nice to him this time."

That same Jephthah opened his mouth and said something stupid and then made it worse by sacrificing his daughter as a burnt offering as if God was somehow okay with that.

In Judges 13-16, we find the days of Samson, perhaps the most carnal man who ever lived.

In Judges 17, we find a man stealing silver from his mother, and we find his mother cursing up a blue streak. Then when the man gave his mother the silver back, she turned pious and started "talking churchy." Then she took the silver and made an idol to worship out of it.

In Judges 19, we find rape, murder, and dismemberment, and then we find the husband of the murdered woman mailing bits and pieces of the body to people all across the land.

In Judges 21, we find them holding a big open-air dance for the purpose of kidnapping women to marry!

It is no surprise then that the very last words you read in the book of Judges are *In those days there was no king in Israel: every man did that which was right in his own eyes.*

This is the time period that Elimelech, Naomi, and their sons, Mahlon and Chilion, lived in. This is where they lived. This is how bleak things were.

This is also the time period during which, just right across the river, there was a girl named Ruth growing up in a place called Moab. Moab was Israel's neighbor to the east, close enough to see and hear and know what was going on over there in "Jehovah's land."

Now, look at verse one again.

Ruth 1:1a *Now it came to pass in the days when the judges ruled, that there was a famine in the land...*

Not only was this a dark time morally and spiritually and behaviorally, it was also a dark time situationally. There was a famine in the land. And it is abundantly clear that this was the judgment of God on His disobedient people.

Now here is an interesting thing to consider. We only read of one famine during the time of the judges, and that was during the days of Gideon:

Judges 6:1 *And the children of Israel did evil in the sight of the LORD: and the LORD delivered them into the hand of Midian seven years. 2 And the hand of Midian prevailed against Israel: and because of the Midianites the children of Israel made them the dens which are in the mountains, and caves, and strong holds. 3 And so it was, when Israel had sown, that the Midianites came up, and the Amalekites, and the children of the east, even they came up against them; 4 And they encamped against them, and destroyed the increase of the earth, till thou come unto Gaza, and left no sustenance for Israel, neither sheep, nor ox, nor ass. 5 For they came up with their cattle and their* *tents, and they came as grasshoppers for multitude; for both they and their camels were without number: and they entered into the land to destroy it.* **6** *And Israel was greatly impoverished because of the Midianites; and the children of Israel cried unto the LORD.*

Based on the years mentioned in the first six chapters, this is right at halfway through the time of the judges. That fits well with the genealogy of Ruth and Boaz. Ruth and Boaz have a son named Obed, Obed has Jesse, and Jesse is described in the book of 1 Samuel as a very old man when he had David.

What are we dealing with? We are still dealing with the fact that it is a very dark time in Israel. Judges are in charge. There is a never-ending cycle of sin, servitude, and sorrow. People are behaving like animals. There is murder, rape, and violence on every hand. There is a famine caused by an overwhelming enemy coming in and eating up all the cropland and livestock. This is the setting in which the events of the book of Ruth occur.

A desperate journey into darkness

Ruth 1:2b *...And a certain man of Bethlehemjudah went to sojourn in the country of Moab, he, and his wife, and his two sons.*

We have just spent a little while observing how dark of a time it was in Israel. Now you are seeing me put pen to paper about a journey *into* darkness as this family heads for Moab. You would likely expect to read about a desperate journey *from* the darkness. But I meant it exactly the way I wrote it. For this family to go from Israel to Moab was truly a desperate journey into darkness.

Moab had a horrible start in life, and things only went downhill from there:

Genesis 19:36 *Thus were both the daughters of Lot with child by their father.* **37** *And the firstborn bare a son, and called his name Moab: the same is the father of the Moabites unto this day.*

This is where Moab came from, the incestuous relationship between Lot and his oldest daughter. From there Moab went on to become a very wicked people. They primarily worshipped a false god named Chemosh. They practiced human sacrifice in the name of and in the hands of that stone idol. They also worshipped their particular manifestation of Baal.

Moab hated Israel. They tried to destroy them during the wilderness wanderings. Just before the days of Ruth, they dominated Israel under the hand of their wicked king, Eglon. There simply was no "light" in Moab; there was only darkness.

For a family of Jews, for a family of Jehovah worshippers, for a family descended from Abraham, for a family living in "the Promised Land" to go down to Moab, was a desperate journey into darkness!

How bad did that famine have to be? How frightened of the enemy did they have to be? How desperate were they to pack up everything they had and move to Moab? This was one of the rare families in Israel that actually knew God. Elimelech's name means "my God is king." His parents gave him a name reflective of the one true God. Naomi herself spoke of God often throughout the book

It is very easy to give them a hard time. It is easy to rail on them for having such a "lack of faith" as to leave Bethlehem and go to Moab. And I am not saying that the "lack of faith" aspect is not true. There certainly was a lack of faith there, but that lack of faith was not entirely their doing. There does not seem to have been much of anyone or anything in the nation giving them much of a reason to have faith. And it had not been like this for "a little while," it had been like this for years.

Yes, they should have had faith in the darkness. Yes, we should have faith in the darkness. No, they should not have left God's place for them, and no, we should never leave God's place for us. But if you really want to know and feel what was going on with this family in the book of Ruth, you need to take all of this into account, and you need to ask yourself what you would be thinking and feeling and whether you, under the same set of circumstances, would have done any better. The humble and very likely correct answer is, probably not.

A diversion that became a destiny

Ruth 1:2 *And the name of the man was Elimelech, and the name of his wife Naomi, and the name of his two sons Mahlon and Chilion, Ephrathites of Bethlehemjudah. And they came into the country of Moab, and **continued** there.*

Take note of that word "continued" and then look back at verse one again:

Ruth 1:1 *Now it came to pass in the days when the judges ruled, that there was a famine in the land. And a certain man of Bethlehemjudah went to **sojourn** in the country of Moab, he, and his wife, and his two sons.*

Verse one tells us the intentions of Elimelech. There came a day when Elimelech and his wife sat the boys down and had a talk with them that went something like this:

"Guys, have a seat, let's talk for a few minutes. You know how we have always told you to love and serve Jehovah, right? And you know how we have always told you that we can trust Him? Do you remember that? Good. Now, do you know how we have also always told you that Moab is a really bad place and that you are never to go there? Well, I know this is going to be pretty confusing to you, but we are going to need to pack up and go to Moab. See, this famine in the land, if it continues, may eventually make it hard for me to keep all of you fed. I know we are supposed to trust God, I know we have taught you to do so, but as bad as things are in Israel right now, if we do not leave, we may starve.

"Now, before you get all upset, listen, and let me tell you why this is actually okay. You see, we are not actually going to *live* in Moab. If we were going to live there, it

16

would be wrong. We are just going to sojourn there. We are basically just going to go hang out there just for a little while, maybe a few weeks or at worst a few months. Trust me, we will not be there long and then we will come right back here. Understand? We are not going to become *residents* of Moab; we are just going to be sojourners."

That was, very specifically, the intentions of Elimelech. What again is the exact word he used in verse one? *Sojourn...*

But intentions have a horrible habit of running straight into the brick wall of reality. Look again at verse two:

Ruth 1:2 *And the name of the man was Elimelech, and the name of his wife Naomi, and the name of his two sons Mahlon and Chilion, Ephrathites of Bethlehemjudah. And they came into the country of Moab, and **continued** there.*

Do you see the change? "Sojourn" somehow turned into "continued." We do not know how many years are wrapped up in that word "continued," but we know that it is separate from the ten years that followed after his death. It could have been ten or twenty years that they "continued" there before Elimelech died.

Back home, the plants that were going to be watered again in "just a few days" slowly wilted and died...

Back home, the cute little cottage that was locked up and had a sign on the door that said, "We will be back in a few days," fell into decay and disrepair...

Back home, the family they had said, "See you soon!" to began to die off one by one...

Back home, friends began to have their memories of Elimelech and his family fade...

This journey that Elimelech led his family on, it was only supposed to be a diversion. They were not planning on being gone long at all. They ended up being gone for well over a decade, maybe as many as two or three decades, and only one member of that family of four ever made it back.

17

Pay attention. There came a day when something happened to Elimelech. Maybe it was a heart attack, maybe a massive stroke, but the head of the home died. Some men they had become acquainted with there in Moab dug a hole and put his body in the ground, and a heap of stones for a marker. Then years later, those two precious boys they brought with them into the land, all grown up now and married, they died too. Now there are three holes, three piles of rock, three monuments to show how easily a diversion can become a destiny.

Moab was just right across the river from Israel. Standing there looking at those graves, Naomi could lift up her eyes and look across the river and see the land that they left for "just a little while." Naomi could still hear the words of her husband ringing in her ears as he spoke to the boys:

"...we aren't actually going to *live* in Moab. If we were going to live there, it would be wrong. We are just going to sojourn there. We are basically just going to go hang out there just for a little while, maybe a few weeks, or at worst a few months. Trust me, we will not be there long, and then we will come right back here. Understand? We are not going to become *residents* of Moab; we are just going to be sojourners."

This family had run from darkness into darkness. You say, "But preacher, if they went from darkness to darkness, what is the difference?"

Here is the difference. Where they were, there was the definite potential for the light to shine again. God continually sought after His people and brought them back to the light over and over again. God continually pushed the enemies out of the land again and again. God continually raised up men to lead again and again. God continually sent prophets with a word from the Lord again and again. As bad as the darkness was in Israel, the light always had the potential to shine again.

Moab had none of that. Their darkness was not temporary; their darkness was consistent.

18

Take very careful heed. There will come times when it seems like a good idea to run from God, to run from His house, to run from His will, to run from His way. But it never is. You will think that it is just a diversion, but it can very quickly and very easily become a destiny. I am glad we serve a God who is able to bring a Ruth out of all of this. But that does not empty out the three graves on the other side of the river.

Chapter 2
There Is Bread in Bethlehem

Ruth 1:3 *And Elimelech Naomi's husband died; and she was left, and her two sons.* **4** *And they took them wives of the women of Moab; the name of the one was Orpah, and the name of the other Ruth: and they dwelled there about ten years.* **5** *And Mahlon and Chilion died also both of them; and the woman was left of her two sons and her husband.* **6** *Then she arose with her daughters in law, that she might return from the country of Moab: for she had heard in the country of Moab how that the LORD had visited his people in giving them bread.*

A disaster in Moab

Ruth 1:3 *And Elimelech Naomi's husband died; and she was left, and her two sons.*

This was clearly not in anyone's plans. (Remember that word from chapter one "sojourn"?)

It is interesting that the Bible does not give any details whatsoever about Elimelech's death. There is no indication that there was some judgment of God involved in this death.

What we have is simply a case where a person moved his family out of God's country and out of God's will into a foreign land, not realizing that he would end up dying before he ever brought his family home.

If God had come to Elimelech and told him, "You only have three weeks to live," there is no doubt in my mind whatsoever that he would have immediately packed his family up and taken everyone home.

None of us know the day of our death. The only safe thing that we can do, therefore, is to always keep ourselves and our families in the perfect will of God.

Naomi now has a disaster on her hands. She has two boys to finish raising in a godless, foreign land, without the help of her husband.

You know she had to wonder whether or not they would maintain any godliness about them. Would they be able to keep themselves from the sin all around them in Moab, would they be able to keep themselves from the pagan Moabite women? O Naomi! If you do not want your children becoming enamored with the women of Moab, then do not take them to Moab to begin with! Moab had a history that should have warned Naomi what she was likely in for:

Numbers 25:1 *And Israel abode in Shittim, and the people began to commit whoredom with the daughters of Moab.* **2** *And they called the people unto the sacrifices of their gods: and the people did eat, and bowed down to their gods.*

Deuteronomy 23:3 *An Ammonite or Moabite shall not enter into the congregation of the LORD; even to their tenth generation shall they not enter into the congregation of the LORD for ever:*

For Moab to behave as they behaved and for God to lay down such strident prohibitions against having anything to do with them, that should have been enough for the journey to Moab to never have been undertaken.

A decision to settle down

Ruth 1:4 *And they took them wives of the women of Moab; the name of the one was Orpah, and the name of the other Ruth: and they dwelled there about ten years.*

Remember that Elimelech had determined only to sojourn in the land. But somehow sojourning turned into continuing. Life in Judah went on without them. Marriages took place, babies were born, funerals were held, crops were planted and reaped.

Likewise, life went on in Moab. A father died, a grave was dug, boys grew up, and girls began to catch their eye. And the very next thing you see, the very next verse after we are told that Elimelech dies, each of these boys has married a Moabite woman. Mahlon has married a girl named Ruth (Ruth 4:10), Chilion has married a girl named Orpah. We saw in verse one that the intention was to sojourn; we saw in verse two that sojourn turned into continued, and now we see in verse four that they "dwelled" there ten years.

They have been there long enough for Elimelech to be described as having "continued" there. They have been there long enough after that for Elimelech to have died. They have been there long enough after that for the boys to marry Moabite women. And then they had lived there ten years after that.

Let me state the obvious; Mahlon and Chilion clearly had no intentions of ever going home.

One of them has married a girl named Orpah; her name means "fawn" or "gazelle." The other one has married a girl named Ruth; her name means "friend." Orpah's name is a clear indication of her physical beauty. Ruth's name is an indication of her beautiful temperament, but later on in the book, we also find proof that she was very beautiful physically as well.

In other words, Elimelech took his children into Moab expecting that it would be easy to get them home when the time came, but those two boys ended up liking all that they saw and experienced there. Sin and sinfulness suited them, and they made up their minds never to leave.

Concerning Orpah, just a few verses later we find out that she had maintained her Moabite ways and desires:

Ruth 1:15 *And she said, Behold, thy sister in law is gone back unto her people, and unto **her gods**: return thou after thy sister in law.*

It is not that these boys somehow managed to seek out and find godly Moabite women who wanted to serve the God of Israel. They just found attractive pagan Moabite girls and married them. These boys were never, ever going home.

When parents take their children out of God's will, they will eventually reach a point at which even when the parents decide to come back, the children's hearts are already gone and settled down in that far land of sin.

Parents, be warned: it is very easy to get your children away from God; it is much harder to ever get them back once you have gone that way.

A devastation to Naomi

Ruth 1:5 *And Mahlon and Chilion died also both of them; and the woman was left of her two sons and her husband.*

There is no indication that Naomi expected the death of her husband, Elimelech. But let me give you another very good reason why they never should have left home. These boys could have been expected to possibly die early. Their names mean "Sickly" and "Pining."

From the time these boys were babies, it was very evident that they were just not that healthy. Taking them into a foreign country, especially an ungodly foreign country, was begging for disaster, just in the hygiene laws alone. A reading of the law of Moses shows that they were literally thousands of years ahead of their time in preventing the spread of germs and disease. Many of the things that they knew took "modern man" another 3,500 years to figure out. And yet they went to Moab anyway. Then Elimelech died. Then the boys married Moabite women. And then, in the final step of devastation for Naomi, both of the boys died.

24

Now there are three widows standing over three graves, and one of those widows is not even from there.

Think of all that Naomi was now facing. No provider, no family, no help, and no hope.

It has all been pretty bad thus far, but the tide is about to turn.

Deliverance in Bethlehem

Ruth 1:6 *Then she arose with her daughters in law, that she might return from the country of Moab: for she had heard in the country of Moab how that the LORD had visited his people in giving them bread.*

The death of her husband did not get her to come home.

The death of her sons is not even what got her to come home.

Many people are brought back from their backsliding by chastisement; I am not minimizing that at all. But it was not chastisement that did it in this particular case.

Let me surprise you. It was not even the fact that there was now bread in Bethlehem that brought her back.

Think of all the many years they had been there in Moab. They had clearly been very well fed there. There was clearly plenty of bread in Moab.

We often expect that when people go into sin, the Lord will immediately send so many negative consequences into their lives that they have to turn around and come back. That is not always the case. The Bible and personal experience are full of examples of people that have been able to live comfortably in sin for a very long time.

So it was not the deaths that brought her back, nor was it the bread that brought her back. Look at verse six again:

Ruth 1:6 *Then she arose with her daughters in law, that she might return from the country of Moab: for she had heard in the country of Moab how that **the LORD had visited his people** in giving them bread.*

25

What she heard about the bread in Bethlehem was an indication to her that God was once more moving in that land and blessing among her people.

There was bread in Bethlehem. There was also bread in Moab. But the bread that Bethlehem had was because the Lord had visited his people.

The Lord would not just have you to get hungry; He would have you to get hungry for Him. Some of you have been hungry for everything but God for a very long time. If you ever want things to change in your life, I mean really change in your life, you are going to have to get truly, desperately hungry for God.

Chapter 3
The Rise of Ruth

Ruth 1:6 *Then she arose with her daughters in law, that she might return from the country of Moab: for she had heard in the country of Moab how that the LORD had visited his people in giving them bread. 7 Wherefore she went forth out of the place where she was, and her two daughters in law with her; and they went on the way to return unto the land of Judah. 8 And Naomi said unto her two daughters in law, Go, return each to her mother's house: the LORD deal kindly with you, as ye have dealt with the dead, and with me. 9 The LORD grant you that ye may find rest, each of you in the house of her husband. Then she kissed them; and they lifted up their voice, and wept. 10 And they said unto her, Surely we will return with thee unto thy people. 11 And Naomi said, Turn again, my daughters: why will ye go with me? are there yet any more sons in my womb, that they may be your husbands? 12 Turn again, my daughters, go your way; for I am too old to have an husband. If I should say, I have hope, if I should have an husband also to night, and should also bear sons; 13 Would ye tarry for them till they were grown? would ye stay for them from having husbands? nay, my daughters; for it grieveth me much for your sakes that the hand of the LORD is gone out against me. 14 And they lifted up their voice, and wept again: and Orpah kissed her mother in law; but*

Ruth clave unto her. 15 And she said, Behold, thy sister in law is gone back unto her people, and unto her gods: return thou after thy sister in law. 16 And Ruth said, Intreat me not to leave thee, or to return from following after thee: for whither thou goest, I will go; and where thou lodgest, I will lodge: thy people shall be my people, and thy God my God: 17 Where thou diest, will I die, and there will I be buried: the LORD do so to me, and more also, if ought but death part thee and me. 18 When she saw that she was stedfastly minded to go with her, then she left speaking unto her.

The case of Ruth and Orpah

Ruth 1:6 *Then she arose with her daughters in law, that she might return from the country of Moab: for she had heard in the country of Moab how that the LORD had visited his people in giving them bread. 7 Wherefore she went forth out of the place where she was, and her two daughters in law with her; and they went on the way to return unto the land of Judah.*

Everything has thus far been about the family of Elimelech, but now we begin to learn about the two daughters-in-law.

Consider what the past ten years have been like for them. We say so much about two Jewish boys, Mahlon and Chilion, and the mess their backslidden parents got them into. But these two girls were very real flesh and blood young ladies with hopes and dreams of their own.

Now consider what their present case was. They are widows—widows who have had a very good marital relationship:

Ruth 1:8 *And Naomi said unto her two daughters in law, Go, return each to her mother's house: the LORD deal kindly with you,* **as ye have dealt with the dead, and with me.**

They clearly also have had an excellent relationship with their mother-in-law. There is no distance between them, no animosity, just a genuine, heartfelt love.

Both of these young ladies also have something else — a family they can go back to.

Ruth 1:8 *And Naomi said unto her two daughters in law, Go, return each to her mother's house: the LORD deal kindly with you, as ye have dealt with the dead, and with me.*

Ruth 1:15 *And she said, Behold, thy sister in law is gone back unto her people, and unto her gods: return thou after thy sister in law.*

Ruth 2:11 *And Boaz answered and said unto her, It hath fully been shewed me, all that thou hast done unto thy mother in law since the death of thine husband: and how thou hast left thy father and thy mother, and the land of thy nativity, and art come unto a people which thou knewest not heretofore.*

Both of them also have a religious heritage to return to:

Ruth 1:15 *And she said, Behold, thy sister in law is gone back unto her people, and **unto her gods**: return thou after thy sister in law.*

I am blown away by Naomi in this. What in the world would ever possess a child of God, a believer, to make such a horrendous suggestion? She is literally pointing them on a course that has an eternity in hell at the end of it.

But consider once again all that these girls still have in Moab. Let me put it this way to make it obvious: they still have *every last thing they ever had before Elimelech and his family arrived!*

They have lost nothing that they previously had. They still have everything to go back to.

And yet, as verse seven ends, it seems that there is very much a determination in their minds to leave all of that behind and go with Naomi:

Ruth 1:7 *Wherefore she went forth out of the place where she was, and her two daughters in law with her; and **they** went on the way to return unto the land of Judah.*

29

The cry of Ruth and Orpah

Ruth 1:8 *And Naomi said unto her two daughters in law, Go, return each to her mother's house: the LORD deal kindly with you, as ye have dealt with the dead, and with me. 9 The LORD grant you that ye may find rest, each of you in the house of her husband. Then she kissed them; and they lifted up their voice, and wept. 10 And they said unto her, Surely we will return with thee unto thy people.*

In verses eight and nine, Naomi is wishing for them that they will be able to "move on and start another family..."

In verse ten, both of the girls vow to stay with her, to go to Judah, and both of them invoke the word "surely..."

It is amazing how "surely" can actually mean surely to one person, but to the very next person it may only mean "unless something better presents itself."

The concern of Naomi

Ruth 1:11 *And Naomi said, Turn again, my daughters: **why** will ye go with me? are there yet any more sons in my womb, that they may be your husbands? 12 Turn again, my daughters, go your way; for I am too old to have an husband. If I should say, I have hope, if I should have an husband also to night, and should also bear sons; 13 Would ye tarry for them till they were grown? would ye stay for them from having husbands? nay, my daughters; for it grieveth me much for your sakes that the hand of the LORD is gone out against me.*

Here in America in the 21st century, young girls reading this exchange from Naomi to her daughters-in-law are going to be completely baffled. Think about it. Girls, if you were married to a young man by the last name of Smith, and he died, and you one day got remarried, who would you remarry, and what would his last name be? The obvious answer is, whoever the "right guy" is, and his last name could be anything at all: Jackson, Jones, Brown, Thompson whatever.

30

But here is Naomi telling her daughters-in-law that they may as well go home because she doesn't have any more sons for them to marry. What in the world is that about? Why would she assume that they were going to be marrying her sons or no one else?

This goes back to a unique custom that God gave the Jewish people:

Deuteronomy 25:5 *If brethren dwell together, and one of them die, and have no child, the wife of the dead shall not marry without unto a stranger: her husband's brother shall go in unto her, and take her to him to wife, and perform the duty of an husband's brother unto her.* **6** *And it shall be, that the firstborn which she beareth shall succeed in the name of his brother which is dead, that his name be not put out of Israel.*

Naomi was basically arguing on this basis that since she did not have any more sons or near relatives, and since she was too old to have any more sons, there was no real reason for these girls to leave Moab and come to Judah.

But do you see how narrow her concern was? She is concerned about the legacy of her dead sons. She is speaking in terms of Ruth and worrying about her not being able to get married, and there was some truth in that. She had no other relatives, as far as she knew, and Jewish young men had been taught not have anything to do with Moabite women. The boys they married had to backslide to marry them. The relative of Boaz later in the book refused to marry Ruth lest he should "mar his inheritance."

But was there not something else other than marriage to consider? There may not have been a man in Israel that they could marry as far she knew, but there was a God in Israel that these girls could serve!

If Naomi was concerned for these girls, and we will give her the benefit of the doubt and say that she was, her concern was only for the temporal. That is a very narrow shortsighted concern.

Look what she said as she ended her speech:

31

...for it grieveth me much for your sakes that the hand of the LORD is gone out against me.

Naomi assumed a lot here, and I believe her assumption was wrong. The text does not say that God struck Elimelech or Mahlon or Chilion. It simply says they died.

But Naomi has a guilty conscience because of her backslidden condition and assumes that she has been judged. I believe a great many times we assume that God is judging us when the truth of the matter is we have removed ourselves from His protection by stepping outside of His will, and we are simply experiencing the law of sowing and reaping based on the decisions we have made.

But whether it was the judging hand of God as she assumes or the law of sowing and reaping as I assume, one part of what she said is entirely true. What she did had affected others, namely Ruth and Orpah.

The contrast between Ruth and Orpah

Ruth 1:14 *And they lifted up their voice, and wept again: and Orpah kissed her mother in law; but Ruth clave unto her.*

Orpah kissed Naomi.

Ruth clave to her.

Let me show you where else in the Bible the word is used:

Genesis 2:24 *Therefore shall a man leave his father and his mother, and shall **cleave** unto his wife: and they shall be one flesh.*

These two are from the same Hebrew word, *dabaq*. It is the tightest bond imaginable. That was Ruth's attachment to Naomi, and it was something far stronger than Orpah's attachment to her.

These girls had the same heritage going all the way back to Lot.

They had the same religious upbringing.

They had the same culture.

They married into the same family.

And yet one kissed her mother-in-law and walked away while the other cleaved to her and would not leave.

These two girls were identical in everything except the decision they made and the path they took!

Your past is no excuse for your future.

Your culture and upbringing are no excuse for your behavior.

Everyone gets to make their own choices, and everyone is responsible for the outcome of those choices.

Why is it that many kids in the projects live a short life of crime while Ben Carson from those same projects went on to become a world-famous neurosurgeon? Because of the choices they made along the way.

Why is it that many kids in meth-filled trailer parks never rise above the level of their poor raising while others go to college and make something of themselves? Because of the choices they make along the way.

You do not get to determine what you come into this world as, but you do largely get to determine what course your life takes after you get into this world. You have the ability to get saved and live for the Lord. You have the ability to keep your life from sin. You have the ability not to saddle yourselves with the results of poor choices.

I got to preach to a high school football team just down the road from our church. I dealt with them about staying virgins until they were married. They looked like an alien had landed in their midst, but every word I said was true and essential for them to grasp. Most of their older friends have already started the cycle of producing children out of wedlock, fighting over custody and child support payments, and ensuring that they will always have a hard time succeeding in life.

Stop assuming that the level of everyone else has to be your level. Go higher!

The conviction of Ruth

Ruth 1:15 *And she said, Behold, thy sister in law is gone back unto her people, and unto her gods: return thou after thy sister in law. 16 And Ruth said, Intreat me not to leave thee, or to return from following after thee: for whither thou goest, I will go; and where thou lodgest, I will lodge: thy people shall be my people, and thy God my God: 17 Where thou diest, will I die, and there will I be buried: the LORD do so to me, and more also, if ought but death part thee and me.*

Let me deal with something that is honestly of a little bit of a humorous nature. These are the words that Ruth just spoke in verse 16, *"whither thou goest, I will go; and where thou lodgest, I will lodge: thy people shall be my people, and thy God my God. Where thou diest, will I die, and there will I be buried: the LORD do so to me, and more also, if ought but death part thee and me."* Where do we normally hear those words? In wedding ceremonies. It is normally a bride saying these words to a husband. But the very first time these words were spoken, they were spoken by a girl to her mother-in-law.

Can you imagine what wedding ceremonies would look like today if we incorporated those words that way? (Minister: "And now, will the bride please join hands with her mother-in-law and repeat after me...")

But all humor aside, look at all that Ruth said and the resolve found in her words:

Intreat me not to leave thee, or to return from following after thee: for whither thou goest, I will go; and where thou lodgest, I will lodge: thy people shall be my people, and thy God my God: Where thou diest, will I die, and there will I be buried: the LORD do so to me, and more also, if ought but death part thee and me.

Ruth told Naomi not to ask her to leave her anymore. She was not going to do it. She was all in with Naomi, Naomi's country, Naomi's circumstances (whether good or bad), and Naomi's God.

Notice the "lodge" part. It was a phrase used of a stopover. In other words, Naomi did not even know if she had a home to go back to. Ruth did not care; she was willing to sleep in the street with Naomi.

The most important part, the part that fueled it all was *"thy God my God."*

Ruth did not "make a little decision;" Ruth developed a set of convictions, and she lived by them for her entire life. And she did so without any help up until she met Boaz.

How strong were those convictions?

Ruth 1:18 *When she saw that she was stedfastly minded to go with her, then she left speaking unto her.*

Her convictions silenced Naomi—the one who had been trying to get her to go back to her false gods stopped talking.

This is the resolve, the conviction, that Naomi clearly saw in Ruth.

What convictions do others see in you, or do they see any?

Chapter 4
Bitter Steps Back to Bethlehem

Ruth 1:19 *So they two went until they came to Bethlehem. And it came to pass, when they were come to Bethlehem, that all the city was moved about them, and they said, Is this Naomi?* **20** *And she said unto them, Call me not Naomi, call me Mara: for the Almighty hath dealt very bitterly with me.* **21** *I went out full, and the LORD hath brought me home again empty: why then call ye me Naomi, seeing the LORD hath testified against me, and the Almighty hath afflicted me?* **22** *So Naomi returned, and Ruth the Moabitess, her daughter in law, with her, which returned out of the country of Moab: and they came to Bethlehem in the beginning of barley harvest.*

After all that has taken place over the long years described in the first eighteen verses of the first chapter, in Ruth 1:19-22 we find an old woman and a young woman making their way to Judah and Bethlehem.

An old place and a new place

Ruth 1:19a *So they two went until they came to Bethlehem.*

I have a very large number of respectable commentaries both in my office and on my computer. What I find a bit interesting is how many of them at this point completely ignore this part of verse nineteen. The vast

37

majority of them pick up with *"And it came to pass, when they were come to Bethlehem, that all the city was moved about them, and they said, Is this Naomi?"*

But that ignores the journey that took place between the two places.

The picture we have before us in the first few words of verse nineteen is one that presents a stark contrast, two different points of view, and should show us in our minds two faces with different things written all over them.

In fact, mixed emotions would be an understatement for both of these ladies.

If you had been watching on that day, let me tell you what you would have seen.

You would, first of all, have seen an old lady and a young lady walking together. They would be walking side-by-side indicating that neither of them was a servant to the other. There would be no servant. In fact, what few meager possessions they had they would be carrying in their hands or on their backs. Naomi herself said that she was coming home "empty."

The trip would be very different for both of them even though the steps and the route were the exact same.

Consider it through the thoughts of Naomi and then get a picture in your mind of what her face must have been like based on those thoughts. For Naomi, this was a trip back to a place she had once known very well, back to a place she had once called home. Naomi had left home to go to Moab. She had left an old place to go to a new place. But now, all of these years later, she is leaving that new place to go back to the old place.

For Naomi, the operative word is old. She has memories in her mind of years gone by in Bethlehem. She has memories in her mind of meeting Elimelech, marrying him, and living with him in Bethlehem. She has memories in her mind of giving birth to two boys there in Bethlehem. She has memories in her mind of her kids playing there in the streets with other kids in Bethlehem.

She also has memories in her mind of the famine that came to her land. She has memories in her mind of the day that her husband, Elimelech, sat them down to explain to them they were going to be leaving and going to Moab.

As Naomi walks, she is thinking of that day. She is thinking of the emotions racing through her as they walked into Moab as the newcomers from Israel. As Naomi walks, these years are unfolding in her heart one more time as she thinks of sitting around the table wondering what is going on in Bethlehem and struggling to get adjusted to things in Moab.

Naomi can remember that horrible day when her husband died. She can remember the agony of burying his body there in Moab.

Naomi can remember the day when Mahlon met a girl named Ruth, and Chilion met a girl named Orpah.

All of this is swirling around in her mind. She will take a few more steps and think of when her boys got married, and a few steps later she is thinking of when they both died and were buried there beside her husband in Moab.

For Naomi, the "new" did not work out so well at all...

So now, as she walks, she is heading from the new back to the old. She has been gone so long that she does not know exactly what it will be like. What she does know is that she is headed home, her actual home. She is leaving behind the land that has taken everything from her and going back to the land that gave everything to her. In the midst of her heartbreak and anguish, she is, at the very least, still headed home.

Walking beside Naomi was her daughter-in-law, Ruth. They were taking the same steps and going the same way. But take a look at Ruth's face, and you will see that the emotions and the thoughts are not quite the same.

Naomi was heading for home; Ruth was heading away from home.

Ruth's mother and father were not up ahead; they were getting farther and farther behind her as she walked.

Ruth, as she walked, could think back to the day she met this amazing guy named Mahlon.

Ruth could think back to the day there in Moab that she married him.

Ruth could think back to the ten sweet years of marriage she had there in Moab.

Ruth, as she walked, was walking away from the husband that she had buried back there Moab.

Ruth was not walking toward familiar territory; she was walking toward unfamiliar territory.

Naomi was going back to a land where people knew her and loved her.

Ruth was going to a brand new land that had been taught to shun people like her:

Deuteronomy 23:3 *An Ammonite or Moabite shall not enter into the congregation of the LORD; even to their tenth generation shall they not enter into the congregation of the LORD for ever:* **4** *Because they met you not with bread and with water in the way, when ye came forth out of Egypt; and because they hired against thee Balaam the son of Beor of Pethor of Mesopotamia, to curse thee.*

Because of how hateful and dangerous the Moabites had been to the Israelites, God placed that barrier to keep them separated.

None of that was Ruth's fault; she had not been involved in any of it. But that did not change the fact that she was going to an unfamiliar land where people were going to instinctively, without even knowing her, give her the cold shoulder and keep her at arm's length.

Naomi was walking toward open arms; Ruth was walking toward arms firmly crossed and clasped across the chest.

Both Naomi and Ruth, as they walked, had an old place and a new place swirling around in their minds with completely different emotions being generated by each.

An old name and a new name

Ruth 1:19b ...*And it came to pass, when they were come to Bethlehem, that all the city was moved about them, and they said, Is this Naomi?* **20** *And she said unto them, Call me not Naomi, call me Mara: for the Almighty hath dealt very bitterly with me.*

The Bible does not tell us how long it took Naomi and Ruth to get to Bethlehem. Depending on what part of Moab they were in, it could have been a few days or even several weeks.

But it does tell us about the reaction of the city when Naomi and Ruth got there. The first thing we are told is that all the city was moved about them.

Think about that. People come and go all the time. People exit cities and enter cities every day. How often do you see a situation in which someone entering into a city causes the entire city to stop what they are doing and take note of it?

This is not a president or king that we are talking about. It is not a wealthy person that we are talking about. An old, bankrupt woman walks into the city, and the entire city stops in amazement as she does, and everyone immediately starts talking about it and gathering around.

How does something like this happen?

Details given in the rest of the book shed a great deal of light on that. You see, Elimelech and Naomi were not just random, poor people.

When Naomi is speaking in chapter one verse twenty-one, she mentions that she went out "full." When Boaz is speaking in chapter four, he mentions Elimelech and speaks about buying the piece of land. In that legal proceeding, he never even mentions who Elimelech's father or grandfather, etc. were. He did not need to. Elimelech was well known simply by his first name to all of them.

This was an influential family! So much so that, when Naomi came home years later, the entire city was "moved" about her.

We often forget how much influence a good family name has. You younger readers need to know that, if you have been given the legacy of a good name, it is of more worth than every single share of Microsoft stock. Never take a legacy of a good name lightly.

The second thing we are told about has to do with a personal name, not a family name:

Ruth 1:19 *So they two went until they came to Bethlehem. And it came to pass, when they were come to Bethlehem, that all the city was moved about them, and they said, Is this Naomi?*

Names in our culture are often no more than a product of what someone thinks sounds good. I remember hearing a well-respected speaker on the home many years ago talk about when it came time to name their daughter. He and his wife tried their best to pick out a name that could not be twisted to be made fun of. They understood that kids are often very cruel and mean. So, they spent a great deal of time trying to come up with just the perfect name, and finally, they believed they had found it. It was something that sounded good and could not be twisted: Denae. On her first day of school, some kid started calling her "decay..."

Names in the Bible were not chosen based on how they sounded or on the desire to keep people from making fun of them. Names in the Bible almost always had some very important significance to them. They were either designed to reflect something about God or the family or that person.

Daniel means "God is judge." Nabal means "fool," and he certainly lived down to that name. People in Bible days would often take up to a year to name their child so they could see what kind of an attitude or spirit the child had and name him or her appropriately. And that fact begins to tell us something about Naomi. The name Naomi means "sweet or pleasant." It seems very much to be an indication that from her very earliest days she had a happy and pleasant spirit about her.

It does not take long at all to figure out the general temperament of a baby. Some of them seem impossible to please, some of them almost seem impossible to displease. Naomi's parents named her "sweet, pleasant."

She carried that name with her from infancy into toddlerhood into the preteen years into the adult years and on up into old age. She carried it with her from being single into being married into becoming a mother into becoming a widow.

And, after all those years, the entire city is gathered around them, and people are saying, "Is this Naomi? Is this sweetness? Is this the lady whose legendary smile and pleasant attitude people are still talking about after all these years?"

Naomi heard that. And Naomi quickly had something to say about it:

Ruth 1:20 *And she said unto them, Call me not Naomi, call me Mara: for the Almighty hath dealt very bitterly with me.*

This is so much more than just black words on a white page. Put yourself back there; feel the emotions:

"Is that Naomi? Is that sweetness?"

"Do not... call me... that. Do not call me Naomi anymore. I used to be Naomi... But that was a long time ago. I used to have very good reasons to be sweet; it used to be easy for me to be pleasant, but no more. Do not ever call me Naomi again; call me Mara, call me bitterness, for the Almighty hath dealt very bitterly with me..."

This woman had a name, a name she had had for a very long time, an old name, Naomi. Now she is giving herself a brand-new name far more indicative of her current attitude. Now she is calling herself Mara, meaning bitterness.

There is both a positive and a negative in what she did. The negative is clearly the bitterness itself. Being bitter is never a good or productive thing. And being bitter will always affect far more than just the person who gets bitter:

43

Hebrews 12:15 *Looking diligently lest any man fail of the grace of God; lest any root of bitterness springing up trouble you, and thereby many be defiled;*

Notice that in this verse there are three phrases, but only the first two phrases contain the word "lest." That word lest indicates that something is a possibility. The first phrase tells us that it is possible for a person to "fail of the grace of God." This is not a study of the book of Hebrews, so I am not going to go into the meaning of that phrase here, I just want you to understand that it is a possibility that is being dealt with.

The second phrase tells us that it is a possibility that a root of bitterness can spring up in you and trouble you.

But the third phrase does not use the word "lest." The third phrase simply says, *"and thereby many be defiled."* The third phase is not a possibility; the third phrase is a certainty. If you get bitter and are around people with your bitterness, people are going to get defiled by your bitterness; they are going to get dirtied and changed for the worse by your bitterness.

Naomi is bitter, and nothing good can possibly come from that. Anything good that is about to happen in her life will be in spite of her bitterness, not because of it.

I have seen some of God's choicest servants ruined by bitterness, and in every case, I have seen their bitterness rub off on others and ruin them as well.

You may remember a moment ago that I mentioned a positive to be found in all of this, though. The positive is that at least she recognized her bitterness and was willing to be honest about it. The hardest person to ever deal with on this subject will be an individual who is bitter and yet is utterly dishonest about that bitterness.

When a person just clams up and says "fine" a lot, there is a huge problem that is nowhere near being able to be corrected.

An old condition and a new condition

Ruth 1:21 *I went out full, and the LORD hath brought me home again empty: why then call ye me Naomi, seeing the LORD hath testified against me, and the Almighty hath afflicted me?*

Some of the most jaw-dropping words in Scripture are in Ruth 1:21, *"I went out full..."*

I went out full. Do you understand what this is referring to? This is going all the way back to the time that they left Bethlehem because of the famine and went to Moab to sojourn.

Let me tell you the picture that forms in our minds as we examine the first few verses of the book of Ruth. We get in our minds the picture of a family that has used up their last morsel of bread, sees no help and no hope on the horizon, and in desperation makes their way to Moab hoping not to starve before they get there.

But Naomi said, "I went out full." That word full is descriptive of everything in her life, not just of her stomach. Elimelech and Naomi did not leave Bethlehem once they became destitute; they left Bethlehem while they still had plenty, fearing that if they stayed, they might possibly become destitute.

In other words, they walked by sight and not by faith. Rather than staying in God's land and in God's will and trusting God to take care of them, they "bailed out while there was still time."

We read of the famine in Bethlehem. But do you know what we do not read about? We do not read about anyone in Bethlehem starving to death. In fact, we read of a man who stayed all through the famine, a man named Boaz, and he actually became or stayed very wealthy during the famine!

By contrast, Elimelech, who also seemed to have been a man of great means, took the opposite approach to Boaz. He left during the time of the famine, and the only one ever to make it back was his wife, and she came back destitute.

She said, "I went out full; I came home empty." She then added, *the Lord has testified against me, and the Almighty has afflicted me.*"

As I said in an earlier chapter, I do not believe that this was the case. She is basically claiming that God has actively taken everything from her. But Job made the same claim when it was clear that it was the devil who had taken everything from him.

In Naomi's case, it certainly appears that she and her family removed themselves from the place of God's blessings, and God allowed them to do it. But God is not going to chase you or me down in our backslidden condition to force on us the blessings He would have given us had we stayed in His will. If you and I want God's blessings in our lives, then we need to have enough sense to stay in the center of His will no matter what the circumstances around us seem to be pressing us to do.

Naomi's old condition was that she was "full." She had everything she needed and everything she wanted. She left Bethlehem and went to Moab, and she came back in a new condition, "empty."

I was preaching a meeting sometime back, and a gentleman stopped to talk to me when I was done. He began to tell me how a great many years ago he had backslidden on God. He knew it was wrong; he knew he needed to be in the house of God; he knew he needed to be doing right in serving the Lord, but he willfully chose to go his own way.

As tears filled his eyes, he told me of how his children followed him away from God and grew up in that condition.

He said, "My wife and I came home one night, and my son, a young adult at the time, was waiting for us. He hugged his mother and said, 'I love you, mom.' Then he turned and walked into the other room. I thought that was odd, but I was too busy to give it much thought. A few seconds later I heard the gun go off in the other room..."

That boy had waited for his parents to come home so he could tell his mom he loved her one more time. Then he had gone into the other room and pulled the trigger and taken his own life.

That man looked at me and said, "I got right with God and got back in church a few months after that. But my son is still gone..."

Naomi could have related to his story. She went out full, and she came home empty.

An old harvest and a new harvest

Ruth 1:22 *So Naomi returned, and Ruth the Moabitess, her daughter in law, with her, which returned out of the country of Moab: and they came to Bethlehem in the beginning of barley harvest.*

Everything that we have described in the life of Naomi thus far is the harvest of the choices that she and her husband made. The New Testament puts it this way:

Galatians 6:7 *Be not deceived; God is not mocked: for whatsoever a man soweth, that shall he also reap.* **8** *For he that soweth to his flesh shall of the flesh reap corruption; but he that soweth to the Spirit shall of the Spirit reap life everlasting.*

Decisions have consequences. I often say, "The choices you make plus the consequences that follow equal your life. Therefore, better decisions equal better results."

Elimelech and Naomi have made choices along the way, and they have not turned out well. The harvest of their choices has been a bitter harvest.

But I am so glad we serve a merciful God who continues to keep turning the fields and allowing us to plant in them. I am glad we serve a God who has no desire of leaving us in our harvest of bitterness.

As they made their way to Bethlehem, there were many huge legal and family and relationship issues that were being presented and needed to be dealt with. But in the midst of all of that, God had the writer of the book of Ruth include a detail that at first blush seems to be nothing more than filler material: *"and they came to Bethlehem in the beginning of barley harvest."*

You and I know that this is going to come into play in the future chapters of the book and in the relationship that develops between Ruth and Boaz. But for now, none of that is in view. For now, at this point in the narrative, God is just telling us that it is the beginning of the barley harvest. That barley harvest took place in the spring. It was the time when everything was springing to life again.

Everything for the last several years in the life of Naomi has been death, death, and more death. The seeds she and her husband have sown have produced a harvest of bitterness.

But now they have arrived back in Bethlehem, Naomi and Ruth, and it is the beginning of barley harvest; it is the springtime. Flowers are starting to bloom; the grass is starting to grow; the trees are starting to bud; there is a sweetness in the air.

Yes, Naomi had an old harvest, and it was a very bitter one. But the God of life was producing a brand-new harvest for them to participate in!

You do not have to stay in your old harvest of bitterness. You can come home; you can seek God out all over again. You can let go of your past, and you can walk forward into the future and into the pleasant harvest that God designs for you now.

Let me say that again: You do not have to stay in your old harvest of bitterness. You can come home; you can seek God out all over again. You can let go of your past, and you can walk forward into the future and into the pleasant harvest that God designs for you now.

You say, "But I am old." So was Naomi. Yet this woman who had been in the bondage of bitterness for a great many years found out that her best years were still ahead of her. If you will let go of your bitterness and seek God and His will in the right now, you too will find out that your very best years can be ahead of you.

September 25, 2009, God took us somewhere we did not mean to be, and it turned out to be well worth the detour. We left out Thursday morning to go to Ohio to pick up a trailer. I planned to take a detour to the Creation Museum on Friday on the way back, then drive the rest of the way home that night. With good conditions, we should have been able to make it home around midnight.

But about halfway down the mountains of Tennessee, all those plans went out the window. A fog set in worse than any I have ever been in in my life; I could see maybe five feet in front of me going down those steep mountain roads. Realizing how dangerous that was, we got off at Exit 134 and looked for a hotel. We found one at the top of a steep hill, a Hampton Inn. We went inside and checked in. On the way to the room, though, I knew I was going to have to come back down the halls and do some exploring. Every wall was lined with old historical pictures, many of them about a family with the last name of Ayers. So, once we had gotten into the room, Caleb and I went back out, wandered down every hall, looked at all the pictures, and read all the plaques. But it was when we got into the lobby that we found the most interesting thing of all. In a glass case, there was an old leather jacket. Right through the pocket, over the left chest, was a bullet hole. Beside that case were two other glass cases, one with a shotgun, the other with a pistol. That, I had to know the story of.

Here is what I found out. That old jacket once belonged to a man named "High Johnny" Ayers. They called him "High Johnny" because John Ayers stood six-foot-four. He was raised just a few miles away in Stinking Creek, Tennessee. He married a girl named Lassie Clepper in 1929, and within a few years they had three children; a daughter named Jerlene, a son named Haskel, nicknamed Hack, and another son named R. L. This man was a hard worker, a coal miner, farmer, and saw-miller all at the same time.

But it was his fourth job that got him into trouble. Johnny Ayers was also a third-generation moonshiner.

In early October of 1943, John purchased a farm in Lafollette and also purchased the nearby Colonial Cottages Hotel and Restaurant. Three weeks later on Friday, October 29, there was no school in Campbell County. So, Johnny Ayers woke up Hack, his seven-year-old boy, to ride with him to Middlesboro, Kentucky. They were making a whiskey run. They got to an area called Ball's Court, loaded up the cases of whiskey, drove back to the farm, and stashed it in a chicken coop. Then they drove back to Johnny Ayers place of business.

Around 5:30, his daughter Jerlene called to say that some Tennessee Highway Patrolmen were in the barn with a search warrant. So, John, his brother Rosco, and young Haskel in the back seat started back towards the farm. On the way there, they stopped by a friend's house to pick up a 12-gauge, double-barreled shotgun he had loaned him. By the time they got back to the farm, the police had found the whiskey. Not only had they found it, but they had also decided to enjoy it themselves on the spot, and they were all drunk. Johnny Ayers sent little Haskel in to be safe with his mom, and he went out to the barn, shotgun in hand, Rosco beside him with a .45. Haskel had just gotten into the kitchen when war started out by the barn. The drunken cops had seen the big, tall moonshiner coming with a double barrel in his hands, and they opened up on him. Lassie Ayers and little Haskel bolted out for the barn and got there just in time for the shots to stop and to hear a policeman say, "I got him!" Haskel stopped, seven years old, and raised his hands in terror. His mom bolted over to her husband and found that he had been shot right through the heart and had died instantly. There were thirty bullet holes in the car that he had taken cover behind, but one found its mark right through his leather jacket.

Little Haskel watched as the hearse arrived a short time later; he watched as his dad was loaded up into it, no sheet or anything over him; he watched his dad's body carted away.

That weekend, criminal or not, moonshiner or not, a community knew that a widow and three young kids needed them. In that tiny mountain town, more than two hundred people showed up to express their condolences.

But when everything was said and done, Lassie Ayers and the kids had a seemingly insurmountable mountain to climb. Tons of debt on a new business, piles of work, and no husband, no dad there to do it. So, she talked to the kids and said, "If I try to operate this hotel, will you all help me? Because if you do not, I may have to send you to an orphanage for a while, just so you won't starve." All three kids said that they would rather stay and help her than go to an orphanage, so they did.

Years later, the Colonial Cottages Hotel and Restaurant was renamed. It is now the Hampton Inn of Caryville where we stayed on a Friday night that was too foggy for me to get home. On Saturday morning, we got up and went down to the lobby for breakfast. There was a nice young lady behind the desk and a nice old man cleaning tables in the lobby. He greeted everyone with a smile, asked where they were from, and told them he hoped they had enjoyed their stay. My wife and I spoke to him; he was so friendly, we just had to.

You know, somehow, I just had a hunch, and so I asked.

As it turns out, the nice old man used to be a little seven-year-old boy who heard the gunshots as his father went out into eternity. The nice old man was Haskel Ayers, now 73 years old. He told us, "When we first had to go to work in the hotel, I hated it. But you know, now I love every minute of it, and now I have two of them!" Then he smiled again and went off to greet some other folks.

I found out that he has been a cook, furniture seller, realtor, auctioneer, served as Campbell County clerk, and then was a two-term state senator from Tennessee, and is now operating the family-owned hotels. I never saw one trace of bitterness in the old man. He turned away from that old harvest of bitterness and walked on with a smile into the life that God had for him just up ahead.

Chapter 5
When Happenstance and Providence
Hold Hands

Ruth 2:1 *And Naomi had a kinsman of her husband's, a mighty man of wealth, of the family of Elimelech; and his name was Boaz.* **2** *And Ruth the Moabitess said unto Naomi, Let me now go to the field, and glean ears of corn after him in whose sight I shall find grace. And she said unto her, Go, my daughter.* **3** *And she went, and came, and gleaned in the field after the reapers: and her hap was to light on a part of the field belonging unto Boaz, who was of the kindred of Elimelech.*

As we saw in the last chapter, Ruth and Naomi walked into Bethlehem at the beginning of the barley harvest, and all the city was moved about them.

But that excitement would not take long to start to die down. And when it did, Naomi and Ruth found themselves having to confront a very stark reality—they were two poverty-stricken single ladies who had to find some way just to survive.

An unexpected kinsman

Ruth 2:1 *And Naomi had a kinsman of her husband's, a mighty man of wealth, of the family of Elimelech; and his name was Boaz.*

Thus far in the story, the characters have been as follows: Elimelech... Naomi... Mahlon... Chilion... Orpah... Ruth.

But if this were a stage play, it would be a very unusual stage play, because in the very first scene, three main characters died and one disappeared. In fact, the two characters that were left would have been considered two of the less important characters when everything began: a Jewish woman and a Moabite woman.

But as the curtain would rise on the second scene, another character would be introduced to the audience.

This man who literally lived and literally walked through the pages of history more than three thousand years ago was named Boaz.

Whoever wrote the book of Ruth did not begin chapter two by saying, "And Naomi knew that she had a kinsman of her husband's." He began it by saying, "*And Naomi had a kinsman of her husband's...*"

When you go back through chapter one, where Naomi was still in Moab and getting ready to come back to Bethlehem, the words that she says to her daughters-in-law paint a picture of someone who believes she has no one and nothing to bring those girls home to. She never mentions any family, she certainly never mentions any near family; she tells them to go back home to their false gods because she is empty and without hope.

I cannot find any indication in the text that Naomi expected Boaz to still be alive, or any other family for that matter. And yet, the text tells us, "*And Naomi had a kinsman of her husband's...*"

It then says that he was "*a mighty man of wealth.*"

In today's phraseology, we would say that Boaz was a powerful and wealthy man. Boaz was the multi-millionaire of his day.

That is going to become very important later on in the story, so just file it away in your mind for right now and hang onto it.

Now look at the verse one more time and notice something that may sound redundant but actually is not. In fact, it is very important:

Ruth 2:1 *And Naomi had a kinsman of her husband's, a mighty man of wealth, of the family of Elimelech; and his name was Boaz.*

What two phrases do you see that sound redundant?

A kinsman of her husband's... of the family of Elimelech...

Here is why the second phrase is included and essential. It lets us know that Boaz was not just some cousin way, way down the line; he was actually of the immediate family of Elimelech. He was a brother or uncle or nephew or something that close.

This is another reason I say that Boaz was an unexpected kinsman. Without jumping too far ahead, you already know that Boaz was eligible to marry Ruth and that he did, in fact, end up doing so. But when Naomi was telling Ruth to go home, she made it clear that as far as she knew, there was no one in her family available to marry Ruth.

The text gives us every indication that Boaz was the most unexpected of surprises. But at this point in the text, the writer of the book of Ruth is telling us that there is a Boaz, but neither Naomi nor Ruth know that as of yet.

An unusual character

Ruth 2:2 *And Ruth the Moabitess said unto Naomi, Let me now go to the field, and glean ears of corn after him in whose sight I shall find grace. And she said unto her, Go, my daughter.*

Throughout the years the Jewish people have been labeled many different ways, and many of those labels are patently unfair. One of the ways they have always been pictured is greedy and moneygrubbing, hanging onto every penny under every circumstance.

But history tells a different story. In fact, there was actually a law on their books that, if it ever was passed into law in our day, would send people into an angry frenzy. Look at it:

Leviticus 19:9 *And when ye reap the harvest of your land, thou shalt not wholly reap the corners of thy field, neither shalt thou gather the gleanings of thy harvest.* **10** *And thou shalt not glean thy vineyard, neither shalt thou gather every grape of thy vineyard; thou shalt leave them for the poor and stranger: I am the LORD your God.*

This was "mandated inefficiency" in business. The law of the Jews stated that they were actually forbidden from being totally efficient in their work in the field. They could not go all the way to the corners while reaping, they could not pick up any of the gleanings, they could not take every bit of produce off of a plant. This resulted in quite a bit of potential profit being left visibly standing in the field, off-limits to the people who owned it, planted it, tended to it, and worked for it.

The reason given for that was so that those who were poor, or those who had come from foreign countries to live there, could work and put food on the table.

This was three thousand years ago. We are three thousand years "smarter, more enlightened, and better educated." And do you know what all of that enlightenment and education has produced? A system that is actually *far inferior* to what they did three thousand years ago!

Our system today is:

"Business, thou shalt be one hundred ten percent efficient in everything you do, because we are going to take a huge amount of what you produce and simply hand it out to people who have never set foot in your business."

Our system today is:

"Thou shalt not expect people to work. Thou shalt, in fact, allow them to go to a party school for four years to study eleventh century Chinese poetry, and then when they, for some reason, cannot find a job with that $200,000 degree in Chinese poetry, thou shalt pay off all of their student loans and send them a generous check each month on top of that."

Tell me who had the better system? Under the Jew's system of law, everyone was expected to work, and the fields were left partially unharvested so that they could. This was an incredible act of generosity on the part of the Jews, and a young Moabite woman named Ruth was about to benefit from it. Look at it again:

Ruth 2:2 *And Ruth the Moabitess said unto Naomi, Let me now go to the field, and glean ears of corn after him in whose sight I shall find grace. And she said unto her, Go, my daughter.*

Ruth is new in town; she is likely still not yet even over her homesickness. Mother and father have been left far behind. Familiar surroundings have been forsaken for uncertainty at every turn.

Ruth had been provided for by her husband, but now the tide has turned completely, and she has an old mother-in-law who needs to be provided for.

So Ruth, Ruth the Moabitess, Ruth the girl whom a whole lot of people are going to shun and despise, Ruth pulls her big girl work clothes on and says, "Mom-in-law, we have a problem. We have nothing and are going to starve if someone doesn't do something. So, I am going to do something. If you will let me go, I will go out and find a field to glean in. I know the work is hard and the weather is hot. I know people are going to give me a really hard time because I am a Moabitess. I can handle all of that, and I will handle all of that. Please, let me go find a field to glean in. Trust me, I can do this. I may not have a good heritage, but I do have good character."

Think of what you know about humanity, which never really does change much. How normal is that kind of character? *Not normal at all!*

I take a lot of phone calls during any given week. I do not mind that at all. But honestly, some are easier to deal with than others.

There is a particular individual that calls from time to time to ask me to help him pray for a job. And the reason he is always praying for a job is because he keeps walking off of perfectly good jobs. And the reason he keeps walking off of perfectly good jobs is because "people aren't very nice to me."

I am a pastor. I am a pastor who has actually gotten frustrated enough during the course of some of those many phone calls to actually say SUCK IT UP, BUTTERCUP! Yes, I have said it... yes, I meant it... no, I have not and will not apologize for saying it, because somebody needs to say it.

Ruth, this girl with such a bad background, had an amazing, unusual character.

An unforeseen appointment

Ruth 2:3 *And she went, and came, and gleaned in the field after the reapers: and her hap was to light on a part of the field belonging unto Boaz, who was of the kindred of Elimelech.*

You should know some things about Bethlehem, some things that will help you understand how amazing the events of this verse are.

To begin with, you should know that the area in and around Bethlehem was really good, fertile ground. That being the case, there were a lot of fields, a lot of field owners, a lot of crops.

You should also remember that this particular time was even more profitable than normal, and therefore likely all the more crowded. Remember that word of how God was blessing in Bethlehem had reached all the way to Moab.

In other words, as Ruth left home that day, there were a whole bunch of fields she could potentially glean in, and a whole bunch of field owners she could potentially meet.

Ruth 2:3 *And she went, and came, and gleaned in the field after the reapers: and her hap was to light on a part of the field belonging unto Boaz, who was of the kindred of Elimelech.*

The Bible says, *"And she went, and came, and gleaned in the field after the reapers."*

Ruth, in her humility, went out into a field that day. The reapers were out there gleaning, gathering the bulk of what was there, quickly loading up their containers.

Ruth was following behind them. What little bits they left, she carefully went through and picked. Her job was much harder than theirs, but she stayed at it.

My mind cannot help but wonder, people always being people, how did she get treated that day? Could she hear the sarcastic and derogatory comments from other gleaners about "that foreign girl?" Did she have to endure taunts and sneers from people who viewed themselves as "better by birth?"

She stayed at it. She kept gleaning. She had chosen some random field, gotten in behind the maidens doing the reaping, and started gleaning after them. By what she was doing, whether she liked it or not, she was announcing to everyone, "I am poor! I have nothing, and so I am out here gathering the scraps so that I can eat and not die."

Everyone who saw what she was doing knew that she was poverty-stricken. They knew they were far better off than her. They knew they occupied a much higher rung on the societal ladder.

But look at the verse one more time, please:

Ruth 2:3 *And she went, and came, and gleaned in the field after the reapers: and her* **hap** *was to light on a part of the field belonging unto Boaz, who was of the kindred of Elimelech.*

I am going to guess that none of you in your day-by-day conversations have ever used the word "hap." What in the world is hap? It is from that old word hap that we get our word "happenstance." It means a coincidence, random chance.

This verse is written from the perspective of Ruth. From her perspective, the field she ended up in that day was just a field that she ended up in by chance. There were no signs directing her to it, Naomi did not tell her where to go, she had no friends inviting her, she just wandered out the door that morning, wandered out toward the fields, saw one that looked promising, and wandered out into it.

And whose field did she "happen" to wander into?

Ruth 2:3 *And she went, and came, and gleaned in the field after the reapers: and her hap was to light on a part of the field belonging unto Boaz, who was of the kindred of Elimelech.*

Now bear in mind again that Ruth does not know any of this just yet. Ruth has never even heard the name Boaz at this point. She does not know she has any living relatives of her husband except for her mother-in-law.

And yet, just by "chance," she happens to wander into a field that just by "chance" happens to belong to a man named Boaz who just by "chance" happens to be a kinsman eligible to marry her who just by "chance" happens to fall for her right off the bat and just by "chance" happens to marry her and just by "chance" they end up having a son whose great-great-great-great-great-great-great-great-great-great-great-great-great-great-great-grandson just by "chance" ends up being Jesus Christ, the Son of God.

Are you starting to get the idea that maybe, just maybe none of this actually had anything to do with chance?

You see, what we view as chance, happenstance, God sees as providence. When we are in God's will, we have the most amazing coincidences!

Is there such a thing as chance? From our perspective, yes:

Ecclesiastes 9:11 *I returned, and saw under the sun, that the race is not to the swift, nor the battle to the strong, neither yet bread to the wise, nor yet riches to men of understanding, nor yet favour to men of skill; but time and chance happeneth to them all.*

But from God's perspective, His providence is waiting to meet up and hold hands with our happenstance. And if we will just stay in His will, it will.

When we started Cornerstone many years ago, it was in an old building, a fish camp restaurant. Within just a

60

few years we outgrew it. We were out of room and needed to build, but there was really no good option for ways to add on. Nevertheless, we kept on thinking and planning and trying to find some way to make more room.

And then one day Dana got sick. I took her to her parent's house and then went back to the church to work. While she was laying there at her parent's house on the couch, she happened to have the local news on. It mentioned that there was a meeting the next night at Cleveland Community College concerning the bypass that would eventually be coming through Mooresboro. We had not heard a single word about that. Just by "chance" she was sick and laying on the couch and heard it at a time when she would normally have been at church.

So, the next night we showed up at that meeting. There on the table was a massive aerial photograph of Mooresboro, and our old church building was right in the dead center of it, and it had a big red X across it. I asked the lady, "What meanest thou this?"

She said, "Oh, are you the pastor? Well, we are going to be taking your church and putting a bridge right through your auditorium."

Well now, that sure is nice to know.

And so, just by "chance," we found out that we really should the very next day start looking for another piece of property.

We did not want to leave Mooresboro, and we did not want to leave the highway. We had seen the driveway leading off of the highway onto the piece of property that our church is now currently sitting on. Back then it was covered up in trees, and you could not even tell anything was up there.

We drove up that driveway and realized that the piece of property was huge and in the perfect location.

We spent a few months trying to find who owned it, and no one knew. I contacted a local lawyer, and he said, "I would start by contacting the lawyer who closed on the deed."

We went to the tax office. I told them I wanted to find the deed for this address. They asked for a name, and I did not have one to give them. They asked when the last deed was prepared on it, I told them, "I have no idea."

They laughed at me, pointed to a wall of ledger books, and said, "It will be somewhere in there..."

Books. Lots of them. I reached for one "at random, by chance..." flipped open a few pages, and the deed was right there! And now we had a name, too!

It was also six years behind on taxes and about to go into foreclosure.

The lawyer who had prepared it was in Rutherford County. We went to him, and he mentioned that he had done several properties for the owner in Rutherford County and this one in Cleveland County.

Rutherford County! We went to that tax office and got his address. He had moved to California years ago. So we sent him a letter asking if we could buy the property. A few days later it came back to us; he had moved, and there was no forwarding address.

Now we were stuck. Remember, the internet was very young. But we tried it anyway and found exactly one mention of him. It was a press release from Lockheed Martin.

We looked up Lockheed Martin and found that they had another branch in Garland, Texas. I got that number, called, and asked to be connected to him. The next thing I heard was his voice mail. I left him a message.

He called back the next day. It just so happens, by "chance," Cleveland County had also just found him and sent him a bill for six years of unpaid taxes. He was very, very ready to sell.

Do you see all of the chance, all of the happenstance? Do you see the one coincidence after another from a human perspective?

But do you see the providence of God as well? How in the world does that long of a series of improbable things happen? It happens because if we stay in His will, His

62

providence is waiting to meet up and hold hands with our happenstance.

If you would like to live a very boring, normal, mundane life where everything is always explainable, you better stay out of God's will. Because if you stay in God's will, and even halfway pay attention, you will find yourself having the most amazing "coincidences." You will find yourself over and over again seeing your happenstance hold hands with God's providence.

Chapter 6
Who Is That Girl?

Ruth 2:4 *And, behold, Boaz came from Bethlehem, and said unto the reapers, The LORD be with you. And they answered him, The LORD bless thee. **5** Then said Boaz unto his servant that was set over the reapers, Whose damsel is this? **6** And the servant that was set over the reapers answered and said, It is the Moabitish damsel that came back with Naomi out of the country of Moab: **7** And she said, I pray you, let me glean and gather after the reapers among the sheaves: so she came, and hath continued even from the morning until now, that she tarried a little in the house. **8** Then said Boaz unto Ruth, Hearest thou not, my daughter? Go not to glean in another field, neither go from hence, but abide here fast by my maidens: **9** Let thine eyes be on the field that they do reap, and go thou after them: have I not charged the young men that they shall not touch thee? and when thou art athirst, go unto the vessels, and drink of that which the young men have drawn. **10** Then she fell on her face, and bowed herself to the ground, and said unto him, Why have I found grace in thine eyes, that thou shouldest take knowledge of me, seeing I am a stranger? **11** And Boaz answered and said unto her, It hath fully been shewed me, all that thou hast done unto thy mother in law since the death of thine husband: and how thou hast left thy father and thy mother, and the land of thy nativity, and art come* *unto a people which thou knewest not heretofore.* **12** *The LORD recompense thy work, and a full reward be given thee of the LORD God of Israel, under whose wings thou art come to trust.*

In the last chapter Ruth went out looking for a field to glean in and "just happened" to end up in the field of Boaz.

And that brings us up to our text for this chapter.

A daily life of godliness

Ruth 2:4 *And, behold, Boaz came from Bethlehem, and said unto the reapers, The LORD be with you. And they answered him, The LORD bless thee.*

The hired hands were doing their jobs. The crops were being reaped; the business was rolling along steadily. Yet Boaz, the owner, did not simply sit home and wait for the profits to roll in. The man is old, but here we see him coming out to the field. Throughout this process, we will see him actively involved in all of the business.

There is an old proverb, "The master's eye makes a fat horse." There is another one which says, "He who wholly leaves his business to others will have it done by halves." (Henry, 263)

Boaz is clearly not a lazy man. There is a godliness about him that extends even to his work ethic. This goes a long way toward explaining why verse one calls him a "mighty man of wealth."

Rich people, in general, get ripped to shreds in our society today. They get accused of "winning life's lottery." And a few here and there may indeed have simply been "lucky" to find themselves born into a life of wealth. But very reputable studies have proven over and over again that the vast majority of wealth in America is first-generation wealth. In other words, most people who become wealthy in our country do so because they worked like dogs, did not spend money frivolously, and invested that money wisely.

That formula is still open and available to anyone; many people just simply do not have the character or the drive to do that nor do they have the self-control to deny themselves the things they want now in order to have a great deal more later on down the line.

The godliness of Boaz extended into his work ethic, and in this particular case, it made him wealthy.

But the godliness of Boaz is seen in a much more obvious form in this verse as well. Look one more time at how he saluted his workers and then notice how they responded back:

Ruth 2:4 *And, behold, Boaz came from Bethlehem, and said unto the reapers, The LORD be with you. And they answered him, The LORD bless thee.*

Now let this sink in. This is not a church service we are talking about.

This is not a Bible college setting that we are dealing with.

This is not even a preacher speaking to his family.

This is in a completely *secular* setting! This is a business venture we are observing. In a business setting, an employer shows up at the workplace and greets his employees by saying, "The LORD be with you."

When people in our culture use the word "Lord" today, it is often much more of a general thing. Scientologists use the word "Lord" as well, only they are talking about intergalactic space Lord Xenu and his handy-dandy spaceship that looks just like an old 1950s DC8 passenger jet.

"Lord" is a term used by so many religions that you can actually pray in "the name of the Lord" and get by with it in many government settings because it is not specific enough to them to point to any one person in particular.

But if you will notice that when Boaz spoke and when his employees responded, you will see that the word Lord is in all capital letters in both cases. Anytime you see the word LORD in all capital letters, the person who spoke it actually uttered a specific name, the name Jehovah! In a secular setting, in a business venture, the boss showed up at the work site, and the first words out of his mouth were, "May my God, Jehovah, be with you today!"

This was not some general thing spoken in such a general way that anyone of any religion could manage to avoid being offended. This was so ultra-specific that everyone knew exactly who Boaz was talking about, and everyone knew that he really meant it.

This was not a photo op for Boaz. He was not a politician looking to round up votes. He did not even know this would ever be recorded anywhere; he certainly had no idea he would one day be famous the world over and that his life story from this point on would be recorded in the Bible.

Boaz was talking on this day just like he normally talked on any other day. And this was such a normal thing that his employees automatically responded back to him, "The LORD bless thee!"

The godly daily life of Boaz had produced a godly business environment.

Let me stop here for just a moment before we move on. I hope you realize that both God and our current culture have expectations about religion and church.

Our current culture expects anything religion related or worship related to stay very carefully confined to the four walls of the church. And the reason our current culture wants it that way is because the devil himself wants it that way. If the devil and the culture could ever arrange it to where religion and worship were actually confined only to the four walls of the church, in just one generation the worship and the knowledge of God would completely die out.

But God has a very different expectation of our religion and worship:

Matthew 28:19 *Go ye therefore, and teach all nations, baptizing them in the name of the Father, and of the Son, and of the Holy Ghost:* **20** *Teaching them to observe all things whatsoever I have commanded you: and,*

68

lo, I am with you alway, even unto the end of the world. Amen.

Matthew 5:14 *Ye are the light of the world. A city that is set on an hill cannot be hid.* **15** *Neither do men light a candle, and put it under a bushel, but on a candlestick; and it giveth light unto all that are in the house.* **16** *Let your light so shine before men, that they may see your good works, and glorify your Father which is in heaven.*

Philippians 2:15 *That ye may be blameless and harmless, the sons of God, without rebuke, in the midst of a crooked and perverse nation, among whom ye shine as lights in the world;*

1 Corinthians 10:31 *Whether therefore ye eat, or drink, or whatsoever ye do, do all to the glory of God.*

It is the expectation of God that there be no division in our lives of secular and sacred. For the child of God, wherever we go, we are to be living out the sacred. This does not mean that we are necessarily to be carrying hymn books with us twenty-four hours a day. It does mean that our walk with God is to impact every decision we make, guide every interaction that we have with others, and be the most visible thing that this world ever notices about us whether we are at work or at school or anywhere.

Boaz shows up in the flesh in the book of Ruth, and the very first thing we notice about him is *a daily life of godliness...*

A damsel to catch the eye

Ruth 2:5 *Then said Boaz unto his servant that was set over the reapers, Whose damsel is this?*

You already know from previous chapters that the law of Moses opened the fields for the poor and for foreigners to come and glean after the reapers. Boaz knew that even better than we do. So the sight of an unknown young lady gleaning after the reapers and then sitting with the reapers was not some odd occurrence. He was not asking what he asked because it was unusual to see a non-employee in the field or the house like that.

That means there was something else that made Boaz ask the question. Ruth quite literally caught his eye! As godly as Boaz was, he was also still one hundred percent male. He was not being in the least inappropriate; he was just stunned.

In case you wonder whether I am maybe just imagining all of this, fast forward a few verses to where Boaz spoke to Ruth:

Ruth 2:9 *Let thine eyes be on the field that they do reap, and go thou after them:* ***have I not charged the young men that they shall not touch thee?***

I am not trying to be in the least unkind, but it is really not necessary to give that kind of instruction to young men when they are around an unattractive girl.

("Hey boys, you see that girl over there waddling around in the field smelling like a horse with buck teeth so bad she could eat corn on the cobb through a picket fence? Do not touch that girl."

"We're good, boss, we're good, we're all good...")

Ruth is clearly an attractive young lady.

A delightful character

Ruth 2:6 *And the servant that was set over the reapers answered and said, It is the Moabitish damsel that came back with Naomi out of the country of Moab: 7 And she said, I pray you, let me glean and gather after the reapers among the sheaves: so she came, and hath continued even from the morning until now, that she tarried a little in the house.*

Boaz has asked his foreman a question, "Who is that girl?" He was basically asking, "Who is she, what is her family situation?" The foreman has a full answer waiting, and in his answer, we find that Ruth was not just physically beautiful, she also had a character as beautiful as her countenance.

70

The man begins, though, by stating the "negative." Everyone has been talking, and word has gotten around. This girl that Boaz has noticed is not a Jewess; she is a Moabitess. She is the girl that came back from Moab with Naomi.

But that is the only negative thing he has to say. The fact that she is a Moabitess cannot be avoided, but this man is clearly not focused on it either because he gets past that and then starts giving a laundry list of what he has seen in Ruth. And what he has seen in Ruth has impressed him.

In so many words he says, "Boss, I was going about my business when this girl showed up. She could have just walked right out into the field and started gleaning; the law allows her to do that. But instead, she walked right up to me and said, 'I pray you, let me glean and gather after the reapers among the sheaves...' Boss, this young lady is really polite; she is just genuinely nice, a pleasure to be around! She did not come out here saying 'I know what the law allows, so move out of my way and let me do my thing.' She was as humble and as pleasant as a field of flowers in the spring."

Then he said, "*So she came, and hath continued even from the morning until now, that she tarried a little in the house.*" "Boss, she started working behind us in the field, she started really early, and she has been at it all day. Boss, I would love to have a bunch of workers just like her. You see her sitting there with the reapers? That is literally the first time she has sat down all day long. She has outworked some of my best hands!"

Ruth was as beautiful on the inside as she was on the outside. She was humble, sweet-spirited, hard-working, unassuming. She was someone who made herself just about impossible not to like.

A departure from expectations

Ruth 2:8 *Then said Boaz unto Ruth, Hearest thou not, my daughter? Go not to glean in another field, neither* *go from hence, but abide here fast by my maidens: 9 Let thine eyes be on the field that they do reap, and go thou after them: have I not charged the young men that they shall not touch thee? and when thou art athirst, go unto the vessels, and drink of that which the young men have drawn.*

The law made provision for one thing and one thing only; it made provision for the poor and the foreigners to be able to go out into the field and do the hard work of gleaning after the reapers.

Now compare that, please, to what Boaz just said to Ruth. If you will pay even the smallest amount of attention, you will find out that what he offered her was far beyond the simple demands of what the law required.

Let's get this setting in our minds. Everyone is in what the Bible calls the house, but please bear in mind that they usually referred even to large tents as houses. In a reaping setting, the odds are that they are all together under a large tent. And Boaz has asked about Ruth and listened to all that his foreman had to say. Ruth is there under the tent. I do not know if she has heard any of the exchange that has gone on between Boaz and the foreman, but I know that she hears what comes next.

Boaz speaks to her where she and everyone else can hear. He basically says, "My daughter, listen to me very carefully. Somehow you ended up in my field today. I do not know what plans you were making for tomorrow or the day after that or the day after that, but whatever plans you were making, if those plans included going somewhere else, then just change your plans. I would like for you please to stay here and keep on gleaning in my fields. In fact, I do not even want you feeling like you are any kind of a stranger or foreigner here. You do not have to hang out behind everyone else; I want you to stay side-by-side with the young ladies that I have here on staff working for me.

"I have some good young men on staff here, but just to be perfectly careful. I've told every one of them not to lay a hand on you.

"Now I know that this kind of work can be very hard and very hot. I have no doubt that if you get thirsty, you have enough character to go and draw your own water from the well. I am not questioning your character at all. But I am telling you that from this point on that will not be necessary. You see, I have my young men go and draw water from the well for all of the employees. Whatever they have drawn, you are just as welcome to as everybody else here."

Do you see what Boaz is doing? And do you notice the one thing he did not mention? He never mentioned her being a Moabitess. And everything that he said and everything that he offered was designed to put her on equal footing with everyone else there.

Ruth understood something; she understood that this was not at all a normal thing:

Ruth 2:10 *Then she fell on her face, and bowed herself to the ground, and said unto him, Why have I found grace in thine eyes, that thou shouldest take knowledge of me, seeing I am a stranger?*

I see something in this moment — a breaking in Ruth.

Up until this point, Ruth seems to have been very strong through it all. She has endured and survived the death of her husband. She has left her mother and father, and with an iron resolve, stayed close to her mother-in-law. She has left the only land she has ever known and come to a foreign land. Destitute, she has gone out into the field and worked so hard that even a male foreman is stunned by what he sees in her.

But now Boaz speaks to her, and when he does, it is with the most infinite of kindness and tenderness. And after he speaks, Ruth breaks. She bows on her face before him, and basically says, "Why are you being so nice to me? I am not like everyone else here. I am just a no-good stranger, a Moabitess..."

This may be the first time she has ever had the experience of someone being far nicer to her than what custom demands, and she just crumbles under the kindness.

73

Sometimes all it takes to break through a wall of hurt and resistance is the hammer of infinite tenderness and kindness.

A defining moment

Ruth 2:11 *And Boaz answered and said unto her, It hath fully been shewed me, all that thou hast done unto thy mother in law since the death of thine husband: and how thou hast left thy father and thy mother, and the land of thy nativity, and art come unto a people which thou knewest not heretofore.* **12** *The LORD recompense thy work, and a full reward be given thee of the LORD God of Israel, under whose wings thou art come to trust.*

"Why am I being so nice to you, a 'stranger?' Young lady, you are no stranger to me; I know all about you. You are all that I've been hearing about for days now. You are a legend around here. I have heard all about how you have tenderly loved and cared for your mother-in-law since Mahlon your husband died. I have heard all about how you left your own father and mother to stay with her. I have heard all about how you left the land you were born in and came here, to a place you had never been before and did not know a thing about.

"Ruth, you left behind the only 'gods' you had ever known because you chose to believe that our God is the real God. You have no idea how much that means to me. Ruth, my God, Jehovah, is going to give you a full reward for everything you have done. You have not just come to His land; whether you know it or not, you have placed yourself under His wings.

"You are safe there; you are safe here. My God is going to take care of you."

I have titled this section "Who Is That Girl." I have made it very obvious one of the reasons why I called it that is because Boaz asked about her identity.

But there is another reason I call it that. Not only did Boaz at the very moment he saw her not know who she was, even Ruth did not know who she was at that moment.

Ruth left home that day and wandered out into the field as a destitute, lowest rung on the ladder servant, a stranger. She did not even know that a couple of months later she would own the field! She did not know that the people she was serving under would soon be serving under her.

Ruth was royalty and did not even realize it. But I will tell you who did realize it; the God under whose wings she came to trust, He realized it. As Ruth walked out into the field that day, others were saying "there is a stranger in the field." But I would suspect that God in heaven was smiling and saying, "Ruth is home."

Chapter 7
Has the Boss Gone Crazy?

Ruth 2:13 *Then she said, Let me find favour in thy sight, my lord; for that thou hast comforted me, and for that thou hast spoken friendly unto thine handmaid, though I be not like unto one of thine handmaidens.* **14** *And Boaz said unto her, At mealtime come thou hither, and eat of the bread, and dip thy morsel in the vinegar. And she sat beside the reapers: and he reached her parched corn, and she did eat, and was sufficed, and left.* **15** *And when she was risen up to glean, Boaz commanded his young men, saying, Let her glean even among the sheaves, and reproach her not:* **16** *And let fall also some of the handfuls of purpose for her, and leave them, that she may glean them, and rebuke her not.*

In the last chapter, Boaz came out to the field to join his workers. He noticed Ruth and asked his foreman about her.

Ruth and Boaz had a conversation. He told her to stay in his field rather than going into someone else's field. Boaz was so nice to her that she asked why.

He told her that he knew all about her. Then he said, "You have not just come into my field, you have come to trust under the wings of my God, the one true God, and He is going to reward you for all you have done and for the confidence you have placed in Him."

And that brings us up to our text for this chapter.

A continued humility

Ruth 2:13 *Then she said, Let me find favour in thy sight, my lord; for that thou hast comforted me, and for that thou hast spoken friendly unto thine handmaid, though I be not like unto one of thine handmaidens.*

In the previous verses Boaz had offered some very tangible blessings to Ruth:

In verse eight he told her to stay in his field, and he told her that she could work side-by-side with his maidens, she did not have to hang behind them like some lower-class citizen.

In verse nine he told her that she did not have to go draw her own water, she could drink of the water that his young men would be drawing for everyone.

And yet, when she spoke, look what it is that she asked for, and what it is that she was grateful for:

Ruth 2:13 *Then she said, Let me find favour in thy sight, my lord; for that thou hast comforted me, and for that thou hast spoken friendly unto thine handmaid, though I be not like unto one of thine handmaidens.*

What she asked for was not some further material blessing, all she wanted was to continue to find favor in his sight. She just wanted to know that she would always be good with him and he would always be good with her.

What she was grateful for was that he had "spoken friendly" to her.

Can we just stop and let that sink in for a moment?

Isn't it pretty safe to assume that if everyone always spoke kindly to her, or even if most people always spoke kindly to her, that she really would not have noticed this so much?

Not to jump too far ahead, but let me show you how the "normal" folks around town thought of Ruth:

Ruth 4:5 *Then said Boaz, What day thou buyest the field of the hand of Naomi, thou must buy it also of Ruth the*

78

Moabitess, the wife of the dead, to raise up the name of the dead upon his inheritance. **6** *And the kinsman said, I cannot redeem it for myself, lest I* **mar mine own inheritance***: redeem thou my right to thyself; for I cannot redeem it.*

Let me paraphrase that for you. "I can't marry Ruth, ewwwww, that would just be icky! Imagine how people would talk about me if I married a Moabitess! No, I can't do that, that would mar, it would put a black mark on my family name..."

This man's opinion and reaction were not an odd thing in Israel; it was the normal, expected thing in Israel!

So, when Ruth bowed on her face before Boaz and said, "Thank you for speaking so friendly to me," understand that it was a bit of a shock to her, and it meant something to her.

Have you ever considered the impact you could have on people's lives just by speaking friendly to them?

Think about race relations in America. Have you ever seen a time where there was greater hatred and animosity between the races, where politicians are stirring up that hatred for political gain?

Do you realize the impact you can have on real lives just by speaking friendly?

We were somewhere recently, and there was a mother and a father and two or three children, a black family. They were having such a great time with each other, laughing and enjoying each other's company. When I got up to leave, I stopped by their table and said, "You all have such a beautiful family." They smiled and said, "Thank you, so much!"

It did not cost me anything to do that. It is just nice to be nice, and it makes a difference in how people view each other and how they feel about themselves.

I was working out at the gym some time back, and there was a man in there who appeared to be in his early twenties or so. He had Down Syndrome. He was getting on one of the machines, and neither he nor his mother knew how to operate it. I went over to them and showed him how to use it. In this particular instance, it was the assisted dip machine, which is sort of complicated to use.

He got on that machine and got all the way down, and I had to use my foot underneath it to help lift it back up into place while he was pushing with his arms. I have to be honest, I was straining a good bit...

When he completed it, though, I said, "Man, you did great; keep at it. You are going to get strong!"

When I was a little boy whose stepfather had just left, unsure of my place in this world, floundering, a young lady who was a neighbor said, "I bet you would do great at drama!" She got me over to Shelby High School for tryouts for a play, and that did not just change my day, it changed my life. I tell my church, "If you want to know why you have a pastor with a flair for the dramatic, you can thank that young lady who had a few kind words to say when I needed it most."

Boaz has been so kind to Ruth, and she is responding with such consistent humility. She has not gotten proud or haughty because someone clearly thinks a lot of her. Ruth will always be Ruth; if she is gleaning in the field as a poor woman, or supervising the field as the queen of it, she will always have this consistently humble attitude about her. It is hard not to like someone like that.

A constantly growing kindness

Please bear in mind that all Boaz has done for Ruth so far has been so far out of the range of "normal behavior" that his employees must be stunned by what they have seen and heard.

But when Ruth responded with her continued humility, it clearly threw another log on Boaz's fire:

Ruth 2:14 *And Boaz said unto her, At mealtime come thou hither, and eat of the bread, and dip thy morsel in the vinegar. And she sat beside the reapers: and he reached her parched corn, and she did eat, and was sufficed, and left.*

You cannot find any of this in the law of Moses. What God commanded in the book of Leviticus concerning the poor just mandated that they be allowed to glean after the reapers, period, nothing more.

But after Ruth said what she said, after she showed her humble spirit one more time, Boaz said, "Tell you what, at mealtime, do not stay out there in the field and eat whatever meager little stuff you brought from home. We always fix a big meal here in the house, there's some good hot bread, you just come on in here to the house and eat with all of us.

"Furthermore, there is some good tart vinegar that we dip the bread in. You just sit here at the table, grab a piece of bread along with everybody else, and you dip your bread in that vinegar just like everybody else here."

I would love to see the jaws dropping right about then. But it was only going to get better:

Ruth 2:14 ...*and he reached her parched corn, and she did eat, and was sufficed, and left.*

Ruth is sitting there at the table...

She is eating bread that she did not bring and did not bake...

She is dipping it in vinegar that she did not bring and did not buy...

Then somebody brings out the oven roasted kernels that people in the Middle East still love to eat today. It was a delicacy for them.

Everybody knew that the family would get some of that...

Everybody suspected, knowing the generous nature of Boaz, that the hired hands would probably get some of that...

But then Boaz picks up the container of parched corn and says, "Here, Ruth, I have something for you. Try this, you'll really like it..."

That was not done. It just was not done! Boaz is playing this about as subtly as a sixteen-year-old boy nervously asking for his first date.

Boaz extended Ruth kindness, she responded with such beautiful humility, and then he just kept pouring kindness after kindness after kindness on top of kindness after kindness after kindness.

And isn't that exactly the way it is with the Lord in His relationship to us?

There is nothing that attracts His attention any quicker than a humble spirit.

A complete abandonment of good business practices

Ruth 2:15 *And when she was risen up to glean, Boaz commanded his young men, saying, Let her glean even among the sheaves, and reproach her not:* **16** *And let fall also some of the handfuls of purpose for her, and leave them, that she may glean them, and rebuke her not.*

Let's do something really quick so we can get an accurate picture of what is going on here. Look back with me at verse seven, please.

Ruth 2:7 *And she said, I pray you, let me glean and* **gather after the reapers among the sheaves:** *so she came, and hath continued even from the morning until now, that she tarried a little in the house.*

It is very important for us to know what Ruth was asking in verse seven, and what she was not asking. If we get it right, it is going to make verse fifteen all the more beautiful.

In verse seven Ruth asked if she could "gather after the reapers among the sheaves." I am going to ask a question, and I want you to think about it for a second. Who exactly was among the sheaves in verse seven?

Years ago, an old comedian made the statement, "This morning I shot an elephant in my pajamas. How he got into my pajamas, I have no idea."

Do you see how the idea of place can be misunderstood in a sentence? When Ruth asked if she could glean after the reapers among the sheaves, she was not asking if she could come among the sheaves, she was asking if she could glean behind the reapers who could go among the sheaves.

So, what exactly are sheaves? We sing the old song, "Bringing in the sheaves, bringing in the sheaves, we shall come rejoicing bringing in the sheaves." And the likelihood is that very few people, especially very few young people, have even the foggiest idea what exactly a sheave is.

Remember that we are talking about a barley harvest. The plants would be cut off at ground level or ripped up by the roots altogether, and all of the ears of grain would be picked out of them. The produce would then be piled together in piles that are called sheaves. The sheaves would then be threshed out to get the grain out of the plant.

In the case of the barley harvest, the law forbid the owner of the property or his employees from reaping all the way to the corners, or even from getting every single plant. That way the poor could come behind the workers and have some plants to pick from and some corners to pick out of. But what the law did not allow was for any of those poor people or strangers to walk in between the piles of the sheaves and pick things up that were on the ground. That would be considered very rude, maybe even theft.

That is what makes verse fifteen so beautiful and amazing and, to the employees, shocking. Boaz commanded that they allow and encourage Ruth to glean among the sheaves, which normally would have been absolutely off-limits to her. Gleaning among the sheaves would be considered "easy pickings."

As far as business goes, this was a horrible, inefficient business decision. Boaz knew it, and all of his employees knew it. But, from a business perspective, it was about to get exponentially worse:

Ruth 2:16 *And let fall also some of the handfuls of purpose for her, and leave them, that she may glean them, and rebuke her not.*

Let me put in modern terms everything that Boaz has just said in verses fifteen and sixteen. "Okay, boys, you know how I have always expected you to give me an honest day's work for an honest day's pay? You know how I have always expected you to be efficient and businesslike and to do a good job?

"Scratch all that. Just completely forget everything I have ever said. I want you to let Ruth glean right in the middle of all of the sheaves. In fact, when you guys are carrying your buckets of grain to the piles, dig your hands into them, and just drop a bunch on the ground, in front of her, on purpose. Let her pick up as much as she wants, and don't you dare say a single word to her about it.

"Boys, basically what I am saying is, if I catch you out there doing a good job today, you're fired."

Can you imagine, can you even imagine the conversation that had to be taking place between the workers?

"Jude, I am telling you, the boss has gone completely crazy. I mean it, he has lost his ever-loving mind! This is no way to run a business, no way to run a business at all..."

"Yeah, Aaron, I know. I wonder if maybe we should have him examined to see if he is still 'mentally fit' to run this company? What in the world could have gotten into him? I have not seen a guy act like this since junior high school..."

Now, we are obviously having some fun with this, but let's get appropriately serious as we begin to draw this to a conclusion and an application. Boaz was not crazy or mentally incapacitated, or some twitterpated teenager. Boaz was a full-grown adult, in perfect possession of all of his mental faculties.

Boaz was thinking very clearly. He had not ceased for one moment to be an exceptionally good businessman. He had just found something that was more important to him than business or bottom-line or profit margin.

There was a person, a flesh and blood human being, that had become more important to him than his business.

I often call this the day that business gave way to love. It is clear from the following chapters that Boaz did not actually think he stood any kind of a chance with Ruth. He was a much older man. But even without thinking that he stood a chance, he still loved her enough to throw business to the wind to lavish good things on her. He still loved her enough to place her needs above his business.

May I tell you someone else who has done that? I know this other individual Who was also a "mighty man of wealth." I know this other individual who had absolutely everything He needed. I know this other individual who had a spotless reputation. Just like Boaz, He was a Jew.

And just like Boaz, one day He met a little Gentile bride. His name was the Lord Jesus Christ, and we were that little Gentile bride. God the Son, who had always done things with perfect power and efficiency, God the Son who never behaved in any type of a random or haphazard manner, God the Son came down to the field called Earth where this little future Gentile bride was laboring away in poverty...

God the Son threw efficiency and caution to the wind and lavished His great love on that Gentile bride...

Then He went to Calvary and stretched out his arms on an old rugged cross, and instead of shedding some of His blood, He shed it all, He shed it all, He shed it all...

Instead of dying for just a handful, just a few of the elect, He died for the sins of the whole world...

Instead of just rescuing us from hell, He has gone to prepare a place for us, and oh, what a place...

He could have had the wedding procession take place on a regular old street, and it would be better than we deserve. But instead, He paved Main Street with pure transparent gold so His bride would have a beautiful surface to walk on...

He could have saved us just for a little while, but instead, He has saved us for all eternity...

I imagine the angels in heaven, in their most respectful way possible, would maybe even wonder if the Lord had gone a bit crazy at all of that inefficiency and lavishness.

85

But He has not gone crazy; He is just in love. He is in love with us, despite our wicked pagan background, despite our poverty, despite our history, despite our weakness, He loves us, He loves us, He loves us…

Why does He keep on dropping handfuls on purpose for us? Because He loves us.

Why does He keep on letting us glean among the sheaves rather than forcing us to the corners of His field? Because He loves us. He has not gone crazy; He is in His perfectly right mind. He has just chosen to love us.

He knew me, yet He loved me, He whose glory makes the heavens shine. So unworthy of such mercy, for when He was on the cross, we were on His mind.

Chapter 8
What Do You Know, Naomi?

Ruth 2:17 *So she gleaned in the field until even, and beat out that she had gleaned: and it was about an ephah of barley.* **18** *And she took it up, and went into the city: and her mother in law saw what she had gleaned: and she brought forth, and gave to her that she had reserved after she was sufficed.* **19** *And her mother in law said unto her, Where hast thou gleaned to day? and where wroughtest thou? blessed be he that did take knowledge of thee. And she shewed her mother in law with whom she had wrought, and said, The man's name with whom I wrought to day is Boaz.* **20** *And Naomi said unto her daughter in law, Blessed be he of the LORD, who hath not left off his kindness to the living and to the dead. And Naomi said unto her, The man is near of kin unto us, one of our next kinsmen.* **21** *And Ruth the Moabitess said, He said unto me also, Thou shalt keep fast by my young men, until they have ended all my harvest.* **22** *And Naomi said unto Ruth her daughter in law, It is good, my daughter, that thou go out with his maidens, that they meet thee not in any other field.* **23** *So she kept fast by the maidens of Boaz to glean unto the end of barley harvest and of wheat harvest; and dwelt with her mother in law.*

Boaz was smitten with Ruth. He told his young men, "Let her glean right among the sheaves. In fact, drop a bunch of stuff for her on purpose!" Basically, he said, "If any of you do a good job today, you're fired!" And that brings us up to our text for this chapter.

The substance of Ruth

Ruth 2:17 *So she gleaned in the field until even, and beat out that she had gleaned: and it was about an ephah of barley.* **18** *And she took it up, and went into the city: and her mother in law saw what she had gleaned: and she brought forth, and gave to her that she had reserved after she was sufficed.*

Let's take just a moment and look at the workday of Ruth. Drop back with me to verse seven and let's find out when she clocked in for the day:

Ruth 2:7 *And she said, I pray you, let me glean and gather after the reapers among the sheaves: so she came, and hath continued even from the morning until now, that she tarried a little in the house.*

Think, please, when did Ruth start work that day? In the morning.

Now look again at verse seventeen and notice when she "clocked out." Evening.

Ruth put in a full day, likely twelve hours or so. So, when we speak of the substance of Ruth, the first thing on my mind is not "how much she managed to gather." The first thing on my mind is what she had inside of her, her character.

Ruth was not a shallow person. She was never going to be a "trophy wife." She was intelligent, loyal, humble, and very hard-working.

Girls, you would do very well to emulate Ruth. Reality star girls famous for their wealth, socialites famous for being famous, pop stars famous for being rebellious, those are pitiful role models compared to her.

Verse seventeen tells us that after working in the field all day, Ruth "beat out what she had gleaned." In other words, she did not just carry the raw ears of grain home to deal with them later. She went ahead and threshed them out right then and there. That allowed her to carry much more usable produce back home.

After a full day of working and after the threshing, we read that she had accumulated an ephah of barley.

Try as you might, you are not going to go to any grocery store anywhere around here and find any product packaged up by the "ephah." You cannot buy an ephah of milk or an ephah of cereal or an ephah of pickles. You can buy things by the gallon or the ounce or the pound, but not the ephah. So, it would do us well to explain this in some modern measurements.

An ephah would be about seven and one-half gallons in our measuring terms. This was enough food to last Ruth and Naomi for five whole days (Patrick).

In one day Ruth worked hard enough to provide for two people for five days. This young woman was absolutely amazing; every employer would be lucky to find someone like her.

I was talking to a man last week as I write this, and he told me about the frustration one of his clients is going through. The man runs a company with 30 employees. Last year, they handed out six hundred W-2s.

Six hundred! In order to have thirty employees doing a job, they actually went through six hundred employees over the course of the year!

Ruth had some substance about her, and because of that, she had some substance to bring home to her mother-in-law for them to live on.

The surprise of Naomi

Ruth 2:19 *And her mother in law said unto her, Where hast thou gleaned to day? and where wroughtest thou? blessed be he that did take knowledge of thee. And she shewed her mother in law with whom she had wrought, and said, The man's name with whom I wrought to day is Boaz.*

Let me describe a situation to you, and you see if you can come up with the normal thing that someone would say. Here is the situation. One person has gone out to work for the day, and the other one has stayed home. At the end of the day, the person who went out to work comes back home. Using four words, what will the person who stayed home normally ask the person who went to work?

Probably "How was your day?"

That is just the normal, standard thing to ask. People may use different words, but in some variation, this is normally what they will say.

But that is not what Naomi said when Ruth came home. Naomi said, and I am going to paraphrase here, "Who in the world has been so good to you today? God bless whoever you worked for!"

When Naomi saw how much Ruth was bringing home, she immediately knew that something far out of the ordinary had happened. She knew that there was no way under normal circumstances a gleaner could gather that much to bring home. She knew that someone had been lavishly kind to Ruth.

Naomi was surprised. She was just not used to seeing things quite like this.

For her part, Ruth had an answer for her:

The man's name with whom I wrought to day is Boaz.

Have you ever watched a television show or movie where at some point there is this unbelievable, jaw-dropping twist in the plot? This is one of those moments.

Naomi has made it very clear that she thinks all of her family is dead and gone. She told both Ruth and Orpah to go back home rather than come to Bethlehem with her because she had nothing there to offer them.

But all of her family was not dead. There was still one man very much alive and well. I would have loved to see Naomi's face when the name Boaz rolled off of Ruth's lips.

The sovereignty of God

Ruth 2:20 *And Naomi said unto her daughter in law, Blessed be he of the LORD, who hath not left off his kindness to the living and to the dead. And Naomi said unto her, The man is near of kin unto us, one of our next kinsmen.*

There are two sentences in verse twenty. In the first sentence, the grammar itself tells us that Naomi was really excited. She strung several things together all at once. She said *Blessed be he of the LORD, who hath not left off his kindness to the living and to the dead.*

To do Naomi justice in her words, let's tap on the brakes just a little bit and slow down to see what is here.

When she said, "Blessed be he of the Lord," she was referring back to Boaz. She was heaping praise on Boaz and asking God to bless him because of how kind he had been to Ruth on that day.

But she had much more in mind that day than just a few gallons of barley that Ruth was carrying. The very next thing she said was, *"Who hath not left off his kindness to the living and to the dead."* When she said that, she was not referring back to Boaz, she was referring back to the Lord. Like I said, she was stringing a whole lot of things together in her excitement. When she said that the Lord had not left off His kindness to the living and to the dead, it is not hard to fill in the blanks with names.

She and Ruth were the living. Elimelech and Mahlon and Chilion were the dead. God, in providing Boaz, was showing kindness to both the living and the dead in that family.

Now put yourself in Ruth's shoes standing there at that moment. Does any of that make sense to you? Not likely. Ruth, standing there hearing Naomi erupt in all this excitement has got to be absolutely befuddled. That is why Naomi immediately said what she said next:

The man is near of kin unto us, one of our next kinsmen.

Now at this moment we need to do something else. I want to show you the difference in two things that look very much alike. What do you see in that phrase that seems to be redundant? Near of kin, one of our next kinsmen.

In English, this sounds very much like something that would be written by the department of redundancy department.

But there is an amazing, gorgeous, beautiful difference between those two words.

That first word "kin" is from the word *qarowb*. It is a fairly generic word. Sometimes it means a relative, no matter how distant. Other times it does not even mean a relative, it may mean just a neighbor.

When Naomi used that first word, hopping around in excitement, Ruth was likely still standing there utterly befuddled and unsure what all of the fuss was about.

But when Naomi got to that second word, everything changed. That second word for kinsman is from the word *goel*. It means a kinsman who able to be a redeemer. We get our phrase "kinsman redeemer" from it.

I want you to remember that phrase forever.

There may not be a more meaningful term in all of Old Testament theology since it so beautifully points to everything in New Testament theology.

According to the law of Moses, there were three aspects to the kinsman redeemer. One, if a person had fallen into debt, their land could be sold, or they themselves could end up having to go into servitude. The kinsman redeemer could pay off all of those debts for his relative.

Two, the kinsman redeemer could act as the revenger of blood for his relative. If anyone murdered a family member, he is the one that had the right to exact justice on the murderer on behalf of his family.

Three, the kinsman redeemer was supposed to marry the wife of a deceased relative so that his name would not disappear from Israel.

All of this was a package deal. You could not do one without doing everything. For instance, you could not pay off the debt and buy a piece of land for yourself and yet at the same time refuse to marry the widow. You also could not marry the widow without paying off all of the debt.

So to recap—in the case of death, the kinsman redeemer would find someone in deep poverty, way in over her head, and in love that kinsman redeemer would pay off all of those debts and take that impoverished person to himself, not to be a slave but to be a bride.

Is the light starting to come on just a little bit? Do you see why I say there is no more meaningful term in Old Testament theology than that of the kinsman redeemer? You see, every bit of this points to our Kinsman Redeemer, the Lord Jesus Christ. He found us so far in debt that we could never get out. He became flesh for us so that He could be related to us. He went to Calvary and paid all of our debt. And He did so not to bring us into His fields as slaves, but to bring us into His family as His bride!

We understand all of that looking back. But for the moment, Ruth knew nothing of Christ or Calvary. All she knew was that Naomi was really excited that God in His sovereignty had provided something called a kinsman redeemer. When Naomi thought all was lost, the God of heaven said, "No, in fact, everything is going exactly according to my plan. Just wait till you see what I have for you back in Bethlehem."

The silence of Naomi

Ruth 2:21 *And Ruth the Moabitess said, He said unto me also, Thou shalt keep fast by my young men, until they have ended all my harvest. 22 And Naomi said unto Ruth her daughter in law, It is good, my daughter, that thou go out with his maidens, that they meet thee not in any other field.*

Let's recap just for a moment so that we can set the stage for what happens in these verses.

Ruth has come in carrying all of that food. Naomi immediately realizes that someone has been lavishly kind to her. When she asks who, Ruth says, "The man's name is Boaz."

Naomi immediately realizes who that is and the significance of the fact that he is still alive. She immediately starts jabbering excitedly about a kinsman redeemer.

And what was Ruth's reaction to all that? *"He said unto me also, Thou shalt keep fast by my young men, until they have ended all my harvest."*

She does not mention anything about marriage, or debts, or anything like that. Her reaction tells me that she really did not even understand all of the significance of the kinsman redeemer. Ruth seems to be innocently oblivious to all of this. That would explain what you hear from Naomi next:

It is good, my daughter, that thou go out with his maidens, that they meet thee not in any other field.

Can you hear Naomi putting on the brakes?

Now, Naomi understood one thing very well. The maidens of Boaz were going to be incredibly jealous of Ruth. They doubtless already were. When she spoke of the fact that it would be a bad idea for them to "meet" her in any other field, that word meet is a rather significant one. One of the meanings that it has is, "to encounter with hostility."

Let me tell you what is happening at this point. Naomi knows about a million things that Ruth does not know. She is already thinking ahead, way ahead. But right now she has enough sense to stay silent and not tell Ruth everything that she is thinking.

The steadfastness of Ruth

Ruth 2:23 *So she kept fast by the maidens of Boaz to glean unto the end of barley harvest and of wheat harvest; and dwelt with her mother in law.*

When Ruth and Naomi arrived in Bethlehem, it was about the middle of March. It was the beginning of the barley harvest. Ruth gleaned all the way through the end of the barley harvest and then kept on gleaning all the way through the wheat harvest. The wheat harvest was right at the end of May.

For two and a half months Ruth, the girl who in the heart and plans of God was already the queen of the field, continued to labor in the field as a poor foreigner.

For two and a half months Ruth, who in the heart and plans of God was going to be Mrs. Boaz, living in the lap of luxury, lived in faithfulness and humility and poverty with her old mother-in-law, Naomi.

As far as God was concerned everything was already hers. But as far as Ruth was concerned she could be content living with very little and taking care of her aged mother-in-law.

In the mind and heart of the Lord Jesus Christ, our Kinsman Redeemer, in the mind and heart of God the Father, we are already joint heirs with Christ, sons of God, we already have a mansion waiting for us.

But just like Ruth, it behooves us to serve now in humility and faithfulness and even in poverty. It behooves us now to be content with very little if need be.

You see, Boaz was watching her the entire time, and he could not miss the sweet spirit she demonstrated day after day after day in the heat of the sun.

Our Kinsman Redeemer is also watching us the entire time, and He never misses those days where we demonstrate a similar sweet spirit day after day after day in the heat of battle and the toil of our labor for Him.

And Naomi knew all of this. She knew the laws and customs of her land... She knew by the baskets full of produce that kept coming home every day how much Boaz was taken with Ruth... She knew that Boaz would be watching while Ruth served to see if she really was like this all the time...

In the next chapter, Naomi will spring her plan to get Ruth married to Boaz. But for two and a half months, knowing that she was eligible to do so, Naomi never mentioned a word of this to Ruth. She could have told Ruth to immediately go request that Boaz do the part of the kinsman redeemer. But she did not. Why? Because Naomi knew that asking a devout Israelite to marry a woman of Moab was a huge request. She knew most men of Israel would immediately say no. I believe she also knew that Boaz would say yes, both because of his godly character and because he had already shown clear evidence that he thought the world of Ruth.

So in Naomi's mind, I believe she wanted Boaz to have time to see so much in Ruth that he would not marry her just out of duty, but out of love and adoration.

Ladies and gentlemen, the Lord Jesus Christ, our Kinsman Redeemer, has paid the sin debt of all of us. It is His desire that everyone of us be part of His bride. But if I could play the part of Naomi just for a moment, I ask you to hear me out.

If you are lost, you are not yet part of the bride, and you need to get saved.

But if you are saved, you are this day betrothed to the Lord Jesus Christ. And the Bible makes it very clear that one day He is going to come to receive His bride. My question to you is, based on what He sees in you, will He take you to Himself out of a sense of duty or will He have seen so much in you that He loves and admires that He takes you to Himself on that day out of sheer love and adoration?

I, for one, do not want God to receive me into His kingdom with anything less than utter enthusiasm the moment I arrive. I do not want to have to go in with my head hung low and my garments stained. I would like to live my life for Him in such a way that when I get there, He smiles from ear to ear and says, "There you are! I have surely been waiting to see you..."

Chapter 9
The Right Posture for a Proposal

Ruth 3:1 *Then Naomi her mother in law said unto her, My daughter, shall I not seek rest for thee, that it may be well with thee? 2 And now is not Boaz of our kindred, with whose maidens thou wast? Behold, he winnoweth barley to night in the threshingfloor. 3 Wash thyself therefore, and anoint thee, and put thy raiment upon thee, and get thee down to the floor: but make not thyself known unto the man, until he shall have done eating and drinking. 4 And it shall be, when he lieth down, that thou shalt mark the place where he shall lie, and thou shalt go in, and uncover his feet, and lay thee down; and he will tell thee what thou shalt do. 5 And she said unto her, All that thou sayest unto me I will do.*

Ruth gleaned in the field all day and came home with a huge amount, so much so that Naomi realized that someone had for some reason been lavishly kind to Ruth. And when she asked who, and Ruth said, "Boaz," she came unhinged. She had no idea Boaz was still around! But once she knew that he was, she also knew that he could be the kinsman redeemer to Ruth. So, Ruth spent the next two months gleaning in his field, and Naomi just kept quiet, watching. And that brings us up to our text.

A reciprocated kindness

Ruth 3:1 *Then Naomi her mother in law said unto her, My daughter, shall I not seek rest for thee, that it may be well with thee?*

Naomi had been through a great deal and had gone from full to empty. Through all of the valleys, she had one thing going for her, one bright spot, Ruth.

Ruth had given up everything she was familiar with for one reason—Naomi.

Ruth had lowered herself to the lowest rung of the social ladder for Naomi.

Ruth had gleaned in the field, a poor outcast, for Naomi.

Ruth had brought home the fruit of her labor every day for Naomi.

No one ever had anyone be any better to them than Ruth was to Naomi. And the automatic tendency of anyone's flesh in that circumstance would be to jealously hold on to that forever. But Naomi seems to have learned self-sacrifice from Ruth. The old daughter of Israel seems to have become the student of the young former pagan from Moab.

The harvest was over. At the rate which Ruth had gathered on that first day, they would have enough to survive until next year's harvest and then some. But Naomi had something else in mind. Naomi said, *"My daughter, shall I not seek rest for **thee**, that it may be well with **thee?**"*

Naomi knew what she was going to suggest. And Naomi knew what it had the potential to cost her. She was about to try to get Ruth married off. She was about to try to give up the only breadwinner in the home.

Naomi had no assurances of any kind that, if she succeeded, Boaz and Ruth would help her any further in any way. But she was willing to risk that. And not to get too far ahead of ourselves in the story, we know how that worked out. Naomi ended up far better off than ever by being willing to give Ruth up for Ruth's benefit.

A reminder of Boaz

Ruth 3:2a *And now is not Boaz of our kindred, with whose maidens thou wast?*

The past two months had been taken up with certain things for Ruth. She had gotten up early each day and gone out in the fields to work and glean. But those fields were not just any fields, those fields belonged to someone. His name was Boaz.

She had carried produce home each night. But that produce did not come from just anyone; it came from a man named Boaz.

Each meal that they ate in their little home was a sign of generosity from a man named Boaz.

The maidens that Ruth worked beside each day, they were not employed by just anyone; they were employed by Boaz.

Ruth was fixated on providing for her beloved mother-in-law. Ruth was focused on Naomi. But Naomi wanted to change Ruth's focus. Naomi wanted to remind Ruth of a man named Boaz, who just so happened to be a kinsman, a man who had the right to be a kinsman redeemer to Ruth.

Ruth had such a tender spirit that even though she was young and pretty and had the same desires as anyone else, she would have stayed a widow forever just to take care of Naomi.

But Naomi was not going to let Ruth do that. So one night she said, "Ruth, let me remind you of a man named Boaz."

A request for a proposal

Ruth 3:2b... *Behold, he winnoweth barley to night in the threshingfloor.*

There is something to be said for good timing. Naomi was shrewd enough to know that. This was "profit taking day" for the growers. The winnowing day was when they finally found out how much they had produced and how much they could expect to earn. It was the most joyous day of the business year.

Boaz, as we have already established, had superb character. On the very first day, we saw him very actively involved in the business. Now, here at winnowing time, he would be doing the winnowing.

It was not an easy process. There would be piles and piles of grain laying around. They would wait until the evening because that is when the sea breezes really picked up. Then they would scoop up shovels full of grain and throw them high into the air. The breeze would blow away the fine, dust-like chaff, the worthless stuff. The grain would fall right back down to the ground.

This was hours and hours of work, as you might imagine. But each shovel full blew away the worthless stuff, and it was pure profit landing back in the pile. It was a very happy time.

But by the time it was done it was also very late, and though everyone was happy, they were also exhausted. But they did not just clock out and quit. They had a party, a feast to celebrate the end of the harvest and the goodness of God. This was pretty much Christmas to them.

By the time the winnowing and the party were over, it was so late that they just laid out on the floor and slept there.

And Naomi knew that.

Ruth 3:3 *Wash thyself therefore, and anoint thee, and put thy raiment upon thee, and get thee down to the floor: but make not thyself known unto the man, until he shall have done eating and drinking.*

Ruth was at home. Her workday was over. She was, like anyone who had been doing that kind of a job, tired, sweaty, and did not smell so good.

Do you know what her flesh was telling her? The same thing yours would be telling you: grab a quick bite, put on your pajamas, go straight to bed, and sleep late in the morning.

But suddenly Naomi started telling her all of the exact opposite things.

"Ruth, go wash up. Then put some perfume on. Then get dressed up really pretty. Then go back to the job site. Socialize with everyone for a while..."

Then she said, *"But make not thyself known unto the man, until he shall have done eating and drinking."*

That phrase basically means, "Be out there socializing with folks, but just sort of ignore Boaz. Maybe smile and wave, but do not engage him in deep conversation, be sort of coy. Until the party is totally over, just keep your distance. We have business to attend to that can only be known by you and Boaz and God."

Ruth very likely had no idea what was coming next. And oh, what a shocking thing it was:

Ruth 3:4 *And it shall be, when he lieth down, that thou shalt mark the place where he shall lie, and thou shalt go in, and uncover his feet, and lay thee down; and he will tell thee what thou shalt do.*

Let me remind you to never inject western culture into the Bible. Each and every culture has things that seem very normal to them that may well be scandalous to others. This is not to say that sin can ever be excused by culture. If God called something a sin, it is a sin no matter what anyone's culture thinks about it.

But there are things in the Bible that are not of a sinful nature, they are just very odd to us. Let me show you one:

Genesis 24:1 *And Abraham was old, and well stricken in age: and the LORD had blessed Abraham in all things. 2 And Abraham said unto his eldest servant of his house, that ruled over all that he had, **Put, I pray thee, thy hand under my thigh**: 3 And I will make thee swear by the LORD, the God of heaven, and the God of the earth, that thou shalt not take a wife unto my son of the daughters of the Canaanites, among whom I dwell:*

What in the world? If a man today asks another man to put his hand under his thigh, there is probably going to be a fight. But in that culture and at that time it meant the exact same thing as a handshake to seal an agreement means today.

In our text in Ruth, we now come across a very similar situation, something that was easily understood by them, but which should never, ever be practiced in our day or in our culture.

Naomi told Ruth to wait until Boaz went to sleep and to pay attention to where he went to sleep. Then, doubtless, after everyone else was asleep, she was to go to his pallet on the floor and pull the covers back off of his feet. Then she was to lay down crossways at his feet. So if Boaz was laying north/south, Ruth would be at his feet facing east/west.

Do you see how, especially in our day, anyone with any streak of godliness would have a fit over this?

But in that day and that culture, this was not an enticement to sin: it was a marriage proposal! This was how a widowed lady would propose to a potential kinsman redeemer if he had not proposed to her.

Girls, you are not allowed to do this today. Ever.

But now let us return to one of the specifics of this proposed proposal. Naomi told Ruth to lay *at the feet* of Boaz. That was incredibly, utterly significant. It was her way of placing herself in subjection under him.

There are some things in the Bible that are currently extremely unpopular in our world, but that does not make them one bit less right:

1 Peter 3:1 *Likewise, ye wives, be in subjection to your own husbands; that, if any obey not the word, they also may without the word be won by the conversation of the wives;*

1 Peter 3:5 *For after this manner in the old time the holy women also, who trusted in God, adorned themselves, being in subjection unto their own husbands:*

Subjection. What exactly is that? The word means "to arrange under." In other words, it means to allow your husband to fulfill his God-given role as the head of the home:

Ephesians 5:23 *For the husband is the head of the wife, even as Christ is the head of the church: and he is the saviour of the body.*

This is what Ruth was asking for. She was willingly offering to let him lead her. By the way, please do not let the fact that she was laying at his feet be viewed as some kind of a symbol that she was offering to be a doormat for him, or that ladies should be a doormat for husbands today. Please notice that Boaz never, ever again had her at his feet! For the rest of her life, she was by his side. Subjection does not equal "doormat." In fact, look what Paul said to the husbands:

Ephesians 5:25 *Husbands, love your wives, even as Christ also loved the church, and gave himself for it;*

A man who loves his wife like Christ loves the church will not likely have much trouble convincing a wife to allow him to fulfill his role as the head of the home, and a wife who allows her husband to fulfill his role as the head of the home will not likely have much trouble getting him to love her like Christ loved the church.

But back to our story in Ruth, please focus once again on the fact that Naomi was asking Ruth to propose, and that the way she was asking her to do it could not even begin to be agreed to by a woman who was prideful.

A remarkable humility

Ruth 3:5 *And she said unto her, All that thou sayest unto me I will do.*

Let those words sink in: *All that thou sayest unto me I will do.*

What had Naomi said to her? "Ruth, go lay down at a man's feet. Place yourself in subjection to him."

And what was Ruth's answer? "Yes ma'am, I will do everything you tell me to do."

103

Ruth was humbling herself before Naomi by agreeing to humble herself before Boaz. Do you understand how rare that is? Not just now in our day and our culture, but always!

Pride is the common sin of every devil and every human. Pride is in our fallen DNA, and even when we try to "be religious," the pride keeps squeezing out through the cracks of our religious veneer.

I stopped to get gas recently. There was a poster hanging up for a gospel singing, a "night of worship." In fact, one of the featured songs was listed on the poster, "There's A Worshiper In Me." Man, that sounds awesome! Oh, by the way, ticket prices are $15 a person, but *VIP seating* is $30 a person.

Do you see what I mean? Pride is in our fallen DNA. Even when we put together "worship nights," there is "VIP seating."

Naomi asked Ruth to lay aside any and all pride. She asked her, a woman, to lay down at the feet of a man. Can you just imagine the reaction if anyone suggested such a thing today?

But when Naomi suggested this to Ruth, Ruth did not react *at all* like a "modern, liberated woman" would have reacted.

She said, "I will do everything you have told me to do." She was humbling herself under her mother-in-law and under her future husband.

And what, pray tell, was the result? Every belief system and every choice has a result or a set of results that come from it. For Ruth, I am not trying to jump too far ahead, but Ruth, because of her humility, ended up married to the best guy in town. Ruth, because of her humility, ended up owning the field she used to work in. Ruth, because of her humility, ended up having a precious child. Ruth, because of her humility, ended up as the great-grandmother of the greatest king Israel ever had. Ruth, because of her humility, ended up in the bloodline of Jesus Christ Himself.

Ruth took the right posture for a proposal: a posture of humility. And when you and I in similar fashion lay ourselves in humility at the feet of Jesus, time and time again all the blessings of heaven become ours. God will respond to humility in ways that elevate the one who demonstrates it:

1 Peter 5:6 *Humble yourselves therefore under the mighty hand of God, that he may exalt you in due time:*

I have a question: do you want God's best for you? Then humble yourself under Him, in everything.

Chapter 10
The Rocky Road of Doing Right

Ruth 3:6 *And she went down unto the floor, and did according to all that her mother in law bade her.* **7** *And when Boaz had eaten and drunk, and his heart was merry, he went to lie down at the end of the heap of corn: and she came softly, and uncovered his feet, and laid her down.* **8** *And it came to pass at midnight, that the man was afraid, and turned himself: and, behold, a woman lay at his feet.* **9** *And he said, Who art thou? And she answered, I am Ruth thine handmaid: spread therefore thy skirt over thine handmaid; for thou art a near kinsman.* **10** *And he said, Blessed be thou of the LORD, my daughter: for thou hast shewed more kindness in the latter end than at the beginning, inasmuch as thou followedst not young men, whether poor or rich.* **11** *And now, my daughter, fear not; I will do to thee all that thou requirest: for all the city of my people doth know that thou art a virtuous woman.* **12** *And now it is true that I am thy near kinsman: howbeit there is a kinsman nearer than I.*

There came a day that the harvest was over. Ruth came home, tired, dirty, doubtless just wanting to clean up and rest. But Naomi said, "Ruth, tonight is the night that Boaz will be winnowing the grain. There will be a party. Ruth, you have taken such good care of me, but now it is my turn to take care of you. Get cleaned up, go back to that party, and when he falls asleep, lay down at his feet. Ruth, it is time that you propose to Boaz; it is time that you ask him to do his part as the kinsman redeemer."

And Ruth, humble, obedient Ruth, said, "All that thou sayest to me, I will do." And that brings us up to our text for this chapter.

A total obedience

Ruth 3:6 *And she went down unto the floor, and did according to all that her mother in law bade her. 7 And when Boaz had eaten and drunk, and his heart was merry, he went to lie down at the end of the heap of corn: and she came softly, and uncovered his feet, and laid her down.*

Compare this with what Naomi told her to do:

Ruth 3:3 *Wash thyself therefore, and anoint thee, and put thy raiment upon thee, and get thee down to the floor: but make not thyself known unto the man, until he shall have done eating and drinking. 4 And it shall be, when he lieth down, that thou shalt mark the place where he shall lie, and thou shalt go in, and uncover his feet, and lay thee down; and he will tell thee what thou shalt do.*

Ruth followed Naomi's instructions to the letter. She did not deviate or improvise or "make improvements" along the way; she just obeyed. She followed Naomi fully in this matter.

And that is exactly what Christ is trying to produce in us: followers.

Matthew 4:18 *And Jesus, walking by the sea of Galilee, saw two brethren, Simon called Peter, and Andrew his brother, casting a net into the sea: for they were fishers. 19 And he saith unto them, **Follow me**, and I will make you fishers of men.*

The year was 1840. The place, Fort Hall, Idaho. Two men, Robert Newell and Joseph Meek, decided to take what many believed to be an impossible journey. They were going to take their families, in wagons, 2,200 miles to what they called "the promised land," what we now call Oregon.

They were going to face off against starvation, hostile Indians, and violent weather. They were going to have to use their wagons as boats and cross rivers of violent whitewater. They would be exposed to the possibility of cholera and measles, both of which were likely fatal in those days.

Newell wrote this in his journal:

"On the 15th of August 1840, we put out with three wagons; Joseph L. Meek drove my wagon. In a few days, we began to realize the difficult task before us and found that the continued crashing of sage under our wagons, which was in many places higher than the mules' backs, was no joke. Seeing our animals begin to fail, we began to lighten up, finally threw away our wagon beds, and were quite sorry we had undertaken the job. All the consolation we had was that we broke the first sage on the road, and were too proud to eat anything but dried salmon skins after our provisions had become exhausted." (http://www.historylink.org/File/5235)

And yet, despite those seemingly impossible odds, two men and their families became the first people to ever leave wagon ruts on what is now called the Oregon Trail. They made it to the mission station of Dr. Marcus Whitman, who had made it through earlier on horseback which people believed was the only way it could be done. When they got there, they were in bad shape and were regretting having tried it with wagons. But Dr. Whitman said, "Oh, you will never regret it; you have broken the ice and when others see that wagons have passed, they too, will pass, and in a few years the valley will be full of our people."

Fast forward to May 13, 1843. More than 900 emigrants bound for Oregon were encamped on the prairie at Fitzhugh's Mill, several miles from Independence, preparing to head out by wagon train to Oregon. They were doing so for a reason: they heard that Newell and Meek had made it through and had left a marked trail, and they decided to follow them. They faced off against starvation, hostile Indians, and violent weather. In one storm, they reported rain so epic that the plain was twelve inches deep standing in water. They said the water cut through the wagon coverings like they were not even there.

They used their wagons as boats and crossed rivers of violent whitewater. They dealt with cholera. They got so hopeless at points that they left their most prized possessions laying by the side of the trail, just to lighten the wagons and give themselves a chance to make it through. They came close so very many times to quitting and going back. But one thing always managed to keep them going: Newell and Meeks had already made it through and left a trail for them to follow.

And so they followed. Over mountains, through valleys, through days that were so dry that people claimed to be drinking dust all day like water. And then one day they arrived, they made it to their promised land because they just kept following those that had gone before.

In the verse that we read a few moments ago, Jesus gave a very simple two-word command. He told some men by the sea of Galilee, "Follow me."

That would not be the last time he said that, not by a long shot. And Matthew would not be the only writer to record Him saying it. Look at the following verses:

Matthew 8:22 *But Jesus said unto him, Follow me; and let the dead bury their dead.*

Matthew 9:9 *And as Jesus passed forth from thence, he saw a man, named Matthew, sitting at the receipt of custom: and he saith unto him, Follow me. And he arose, and followed him.*

Matthew 16:24 *Then said Jesus unto his disciples, If any man will come after me, let him deny himself, and take up his cross, and follow me.*

Matthew 19:21 *Jesus said unto him, If thou wilt be perfect, go and sell that thou hast, and give to the poor, and*

110

thou shalt have treasure in heaven: and come and follow me.

Mark 2:14 *And as he passed by, he saw Levi the son of Alphaeus sitting at the receipt of custom, and said unto him, Follow me. And he arose and followed him.*

Mark 8:34 *And when he had called the people unto him with his disciples also, he said unto them, Whosoever will come after me, let him deny himself, and take up his cross, and follow me.*

Mark 10:21 *Then Jesus beholding him loved him, and said unto him, One thing thou lackest: go thy way, sell whatsoever thou hast, and give to the poor, and thou shalt have treasure in heaven: and come, take up the cross, and follow me.*

Luke 5:27 *And after these things he went forth, and saw a publican, named Levi, sitting at the receipt of custom: and he said unto him, Follow me.*

Luke 9:23 *And he said to them all, If any man will come after me, let him deny himself, and take up his cross daily, and follow me.*

Luke 9:59 *And he said unto another, Follow me. But he said, Lord, suffer me first to go and bury my father.*

Luke 18:22 *Now when Jesus heard these things, he said unto him, Yet lackest thou one thing: sell all that thou hast, and distribute unto the poor, and thou shalt have treasure in heaven: and come, follow me.*

John 1:43 *The day following Jesus would go forth into Galilee, and findeth Philip, and saith unto him, Follow me.*

John 10:27 *My sheep hear my voice, and I know them, and they follow me:*

John 12:26 *If any man serve me, let him follow me; and where I am, there shall also my servant be: if any man serve me, him will my Father honour.*

John 13:36 *Simon Peter said unto him, Lord, whither goest thou? Jesus answered him, Whither I go, thou canst not follow me now; but thou shalt follow me afterwards.*

John 21:19 *This spake he, signifying by what death he should glorify God. And when he had spoken this, he saith unto him, Follow me.*

Jesus had an expectation, the same expectation that Naomi had of Ruth. That expectation was total obedience; that expectation was for people to actually follow Him, and it was for her benefit, and it is for our benefit.

God expects us to be actual followers of Christ. He expects us to climb the mountains and brave the valleys and swim the rivers and wade through the arrows and face the problems and just keep going and going and going until we reach our promised land. He has gone before us, He has suffered before us, and He expects us to walk in the trail He walked. We are supposed to be actual followers of Jesus.

Ruth got that concept. Her obedience was a *total obedience.*

A troubling encounter

Ruth 3:8 *And it came to pass at midnight, that the man was afraid, and turned himself: and, behold, a woman lay at his feet.*

Put yourself in godly (and sleepy) Boaz' place right here. Boaz has been working long, hot, hard hours, not just for days, but for weeks on end. This particular work day has stretched long into the night. And though he is going to bed happy, he is also going to bed exhausted. And yet, despite that sheer exhaustion, something snaps him awake at the stroke of midnight. There, laying in the darkness, he realizes in horror that some unknown figure is laying at his feet.

A trembling request

Ruth 3:9 *And he said, Who art thou? And she answered, I am Ruth thine handmaid: spread therefore thy skirt over thine handmaid; for thou art a near kinsman.*

Ruth thine *handmaid*...

Here is yet one more example of the amazing humility and priceless character of sweet Ruth. This is a

112

woman proclaiming herself to be the handmaid of a man; and not just any man, a foreigner. One from a race who normally despised her race. Oh, for such a humility to permeate Christianity today!

When Boaz spoke and Ruth answered, she asked him to spread his skirt over her. The skirt was the edge of the garment that he would have been wearing. It had another name: the wing. It is the Hebrew word *kanaph*. Let me show you where else it was used:

Ruth 2:12 *The LORD recompense thy work, and a full reward be given thee of the LORD God of Israel, under whose **wings** thou art come to trust.*

Boaz had blessed Ruth, noting that God was going to bless her since she, a former pagan, had placed herself under His wings. This word was used as a symbol of protection, just like in the world of birds, when a mother bird will cover her chicks to shield them from the storm.

Ruth used that same word. Ruth was saying, "Sir, you noticed that I had placed myself under the wings of Jehovah. That God has made provision for me in His law. As such, I am asking to be placed under your wing just as I have come under His wings."

Then she said, *"For thou art a near kinsman."* "Boaz, I know who you are, and you know who I am. You have the right to take me to yourself; you are the one who can be my kinsman redeemer."

A terrifying twist

Ruth 3:10 *And he said, Blessed be thou of the LORD, my daughter: for thou hast shewed more kindness in the latter end than at the beginning, inasmuch as thou followedst not young men, whether poor or rich.* **11** *And now, my daughter, fear not; I will do to thee all that thou requirest: for all the city of my people doth know that thou art a virtuous woman.* **12** *And now it is true that I am thy near kinsman: howbeit there is a kinsman nearer than I.*

There is much to see in Boaz's words to Ruth. Blessed be thou of the Lord is perfectly understandable. But in the veiled phrase that follows there is a treasury of knowledge and character.

Boaz said, "Ruth, you have showed more kindness in the latter end then at the beginning, because you did not follow after one of the young men, whether rich or poor."

Boaz was, in these words, bringing the first affection of Ruth full circle.

Many years before, Ruth, minding her own business in Moab, had met a young man named Mahlon. Foreigner though he was, Ruth loved him. When he proposed, she said yes. And for ten years, according to the testimony of the boy's mother, her mother-in-law, Naomi, she had loved him as well as any wife ever loved a man. This despite the fact that he was clearly not a well man.

And then her husband died. No one anywhere would likely have faulted Ruth for moving on with a Moabite man the next time around.

But Ruth stayed true to her husband by staying with Naomi.

Fast forward to the time that they came to Bethlehem, Naomi's town, Mahlon's country. Ruth now had access to any number of potential suitors. Yes, there would be roadblocks; many of them would never have anything to do with a Moabitess. But since Ruth was a beautiful woman with an even more beautiful spirit, some man of Israel would have taken her. Some young man, especially, would jump at the chance for such a physically attractive mate.

But Ruth would have none of that. If there was no relative, no kinsman redeemer, she would stay single. You see, if a kinsman redeemer married her and had a child with her, that child would be regarded as the child of her dead husband, thus ensuring that his name would never be blotted out from Israel.

Boaz knew this. He knew this was why young Ruth had spurned any advances from any young men and was

114

now, instead, proposing to him. Yes, she loved him, but she was also loyal to the memory of her late husband. And if she would be that loyal to Mahlon, she would also be that loyal to Boaz.

Boaz had a keeper, and he knew it. But he also knew something that Ruth did not know:

Ruth 3:10 12 *And now it is true that I am thy near kinsman: howbeit there is a kinsman nearer than I.*

Boaz had already agreed to do as Ruth asked; he had already said yes to her proposal. But then the other shoe dropped, and it landed with a thud in Ruth's heart; someone else had first rights to her!

That she would marry this other man if he agreed to it, Boaz had no doubt. Even if he were an ogre, even if she faced a life of misery, Ruth, out of sheer loyalty to her late husband, would marry him. But Boaz by this time had a fire burning in his heart, and it was not about to be put out.

Chapter 11
A Few More Hours at His Feet

Ruth 3:13 *Tarry this night, and it shall be in the morning, that if he will perform unto thee the part of a kinsman, well; let him do the kinsman's part: but if he will not do the part of a kinsman to thee, then will I do the part of a kinsman to thee, as the LORD liveth: lie down until the morning. 14 And she lay at his feet until the morning: and she rose up before one could know another. And he said, Let it not be known that a woman came into the floor.*

A finalization on the morrow

We are considering in this chapter just two short verses of Scripture, just a few words in this beautiful four-chapter story.

And truthfully, these verses normally seem to get regarded merely as filler material. This is looked at mostly as something to take up the time until we can get to the "good stuff."

But pay careful attention—these are two of the most beautiful verses in the entire book. Do not dare ever skim over these verses. Do not ever deprive yourself of the treasure found in Ruth 3:13-14.

We are looking first of all at a finalization on the morrow. Look one more time at what Boaz told Ruth after she identified herself and told him why she was there.

*Ruth 3:13 Tarry this night, and it shall be in the morning, that **if he will perform unto thee the part of a kinsman, well; let him do the kinsman's part: but if he will not do the part of a kinsman to thee, then will I do the part of a kinsman to thee...***

We looked just one verse earlier at the fact that Ruth had her entire world turned upside down in a moment of time. Boaz had just told her that he would be thrilled to marry her...

And then in the very next breath, he told her that there was someone in line ahead of him. Can you even imagine all of the thoughts and possibilities that were running through Ruth's mind at that moment, concerning this other man that she did not know?

It would be fair to say that Ruth was in a state of great uncertainty at that moment. But it would be equally fair to say that by the end of verse thirteen she was in somewhat of a state of absolute certainty.

I meant that exactly like I said it, and I stand behind it. Let me explain what I mean.

Here is what Ruth did not know. Ruth did not know at that moment who this other kinsman was. But here is what Ruth did know: Ruth knew that she was about to be married!

Ruth knew that one way or the other, God had provided her a kinsman redeemer.

Ruth knew that one way or the other, all of her debts and the debts of her family were about to be paid in full.

Ruth knew that one way or the other, she was not going to spend her life alone.

Ruth knew that one way or the other, she was not going to have to glean in the fields anymore.

Ruth knew that one way or the other, children were probably on the way, and the memory of her late husband would not be blotted out.

It was no longer a matter of whether or not she would ever have a chance to be married. That issue was now settled; Ruth was going to get married! A couple of chapters earlier Naomi had basically told her that that was never a possibility if she came home to Bethlehem with her. Now an impossibility has become a certainty, and Ruth is about to get married.

Do you not love it when God turns the improbable and impossible into the imminent? Do you not love it when the world says it cannot be done, and God turns right around and does it? Do you not love it when the world looks at Christians with an arrogant pity and pats us on the head because of "how hard we have it serving the Lord," and yet God turns right around and moves heaven and earth on our behalf?

Ruth was laying there in the darkness having done everything that Naomi asked her to do, and Boaz told her that she would have a finalization on the morrow.

A few more hours at his feet

I have been excited to get to this point for chapters and chapters now. Let us look at these two verses one more time; I want you to notice something.

Ruth 3:13 *Tarry this night, and it shall be in the morning, that if he will perform unto thee the part of a kinsman, well; let him do the kinsman's part: but if he will not do the part of a kinsman to thee, then will I do the part of a kinsman to thee, as the LORD liveth:* **lie down until the morning.** 14 *And* **she lay at his feet until the morning***: and she rose up before one could know another. And he said, Let it not be known that a woman came into the floor.*

Here we have those few hours of "filler material time" that are not actually filler material at all.

Let's backtrack just for a moment or two and let me remind you of a few things. In the book of Ruth, we have a Gentile girl over her head in debt.

In the book of Ruth, we have that Gentile girl coming to trust in the God of Israel.

In the book of Ruth, we have a wealthy, godly, powerful Jewish man named Boaz.

119

In the book of Ruth, we have this man named Boaz, who has the legal right to be a kinsman redeemer to that little Gentile girl. He has the right to take her to himself.

In the book of Ruth, we have this man named Boaz, who loves that little Gentile girl but would never dream of pressuring her into a relationship.

In the book of Ruth, we have this man named Boaz standing back and lavishing one kindness upon another on this Gentile girl, winning her heart through his love and mercy and grace.

In the book of Ruth, we have this Gentile girl named Ruth following some really good counsel and laying herself down at the feet of Boaz.

In the book of Ruth, we have Boaz asking, "Who's there at my feet?"

In the book of Ruth, we have Ruth answering, "It's me, Ruth, take me under your wing. Make me your bride."

In the book of Ruth, we have Boaz, a man whom everyone would say could do far better than a *Gentile* bride.

But in the book of Ruth, we have Boaz, a man who really could do better than a Gentile bride, saying, "I will do everything that you have asked me to do."

And then in the book of Ruth, we have Boaz saying to Ruth, "I intend to marry you tomorrow. But for the next few hours, just stay here safely at my feet. Do not go out there into the darkness, you do not know who or what may be out there. There is no safer place for you than where you are right now, so for the next few hours my dear Gentile bride, just stay here at my feet, because tomorrow I intend to marry you."

Are you starting to get the picture?

Once upon a time, there was this Gentile bride, and we were her.

We, that Gentile bride, ended up in debt so far over our head we could never pay it.

But one day we heard about this Jew who loved us, and we came to trust under His wings, and we went out to glean in His fields.

120

And then one day the Holy Ghost gave us the best possible advice: lay yourselves down at His feet.

And we did. And that Jew, the Lord Jesus Christ, looked down at us and said, "Who's down there?" Oh, He knew, He just likes to hear our voice.

And we said, "It's us, Lord; it's the little Gentile that doesn't deserve anything. But Lord, you have been so kind to us, so good, that we sure would love to be your bride. Lord, would you take us as your bride? Would you let us stay with you forever?"

And the Lord said, "I will do everything you have asked me to do. Tomorrow, you and I are going to get married. But for now, just lay right there and spend a few more hours at my feet. There is no safer place for you anywhere in this wicked old world than right there at my feet. Just spend a few more hours there at my feet, and by tomorrow you'll be at my side not for a few hours, but forever!"

Friends, I do not know if you truly grasp this, but there is a wedding day coming;

Revelation 21:9 *And there came unto me one of the seven angels which had the seven vials full of the seven last plagues, and talked with me, saying, Come hither, I will shew thee the bride, the Lamb's wife.*

God has his people, Israel, but He also has His bride, the church:

Ephesians 5:25 *Husbands, love your wives, even as Christ also loved the church, and gave himself for it; 26 That he might sanctify and cleanse it with the washing of water by the word, 27 That he might present it to himself a glorious church, not having spot, or wrinkle, or any such thing; but that it should be holy and without blemish. 28 So ought men to love their wives as their own bodies. He that loveth his wife loveth himself. 29 For no man ever yet hated his own flesh; but nourisheth and cherisheth it, even as the Lord the church: 30 For we are members of his body, of his flesh, and of his bones. 31 For this cause shall a man leave his father and mother, and shall be joined unto his wife, and* *they two shall be one flesh.* **32** *This is a great mystery: but I speak concerning Christ and the church.*

He is talking about marriage. Not just the marriage between a man and a woman, but the marriage of Christ and His church, His bride.

All we are waiting for now is that trumpet summoning us to the wedding. But in the meantime, we are just spending a few more hours at His feet.

Every time we open His word, we are just spending a few more hours at His feet until wedding day.

Every time we kneel in prayer, we are just spending a few more hours at His feet until wedding day.

Every time we come to church, we are just spending a few more hours at His feet until wedding day.

Every time we open the hymn book and sing of how glorious He is, we are just spending a few more hours at His feet until wedding day.

Every time we get up and go about our day living as a Christian in the middle of a non-Christian world, we are just spending a few more hours at His feet until wedding day.

Oh, He could have saved us, betrothed us to Himself, and then not had anything else to do with us until the wedding day, but that is just not how He is. He is not going to send us out into that cold night of danger alone; He would rather keep us right there at His feet safe and secure and warm until the wedding day.

You know what? Ruth spent the next few hours in the dark. She could not see him, but she could hear every breath that he took.

I cannot help but wonder how many times during the night did she whisper sort of quietly, "Boaz? Are you asleep?" I can pretty much guarantee you that if she did, she got the same answer every single time, "No, sweetheart, I am not asleep. I am never going to go to sleep with you there at my feet. As long as you are there, I'll be wide-awake making sure everything is okay."

Oh, by the way, one more small detail. Did you happen to notice the end of verse fourteen?

Ruth 3:14 *And she lay at his feet until the morning: and she rose up before one could know another. And he said, Let it not be known that a woman came into the floor.*

Do you understand what that means? The night before her wedding day, Ruth lay at Boaz's feet all night. And then, without anybody even seeing it, she left. She was gone without a trace, and no one even saw her go. That sounds remarkably similar to something we read in the New Testament:

1 Corinthians 15:51 *Behold, I shew you a mystery; We shall not all sleep, but we shall all be changed,* **52** *In a moment, in the twinkling of an eye, at the last trump: for the trumpet shall sound, and the dead shall be raised incorruptible, and we shall be changed.*

We, the saved, are laying at the feet of Jesus waiting for the wedding day. And when that day comes, we are going to disappear, and the world will not even see us go! We will be arrayed in white and halfway down the aisle to meet Him before the world even realizes we are not here anymore.

We are just spending a few more hours at his feet until that moment!

Chapter 12
Man on a Mission

Ruth 3:15 *Also he said, Bring the vail that thou hast upon thee, and hold it. And when she held it, he measured six measures of barley, and laid it on her: and she went into the city.* **16** *And when she came to her mother in law, she said, Who art thou, my daughter? And she told her all that the man had done to her.* **17** *And she said, These six measures of barley gave he me; for he said to me, Go not empty unto thy mother in law.* **18** *Then said she, Sit still, my daughter, until thou know how the matter will fall: for the man will not be in rest, until he have finished the thing this day.*

The few hours laying quietly at the feet of Boaz finally came to an end. Now the action was going to pick up to a break-neck pace. But not before Boaz sent Ruth home with a tangible reminder of his love and intentions.

A significant gift

Ruth 3:15 *Also he said, Bring the vail that thou hast upon thee, and hold it. And when she held it, he measured six measures of barley, and laid it on her: and she went into the city.*

This gift was incredibly significant to Boaz. It was not significant because of the amount; it was just a few dollars' worth at best. No, it was significant because he did

125

not know if this was a "from now on" gift or a "goodbye" gift. That was yet to be determined. That would be settled at the city gate. If a man could be talked out of taking Ruth, the gift he was giving would be a "from now on" gift. But if the man asserted his right and took her hand in marriage, this would be a "goodbye" gift. Boaz, at this point, literally did not know which way it would go.

This was also a significant gift because it was exactly twice what she gleaned on her first day with him. That measurement worked out to seven and one half gallons, this one worked out to fifteen gallons. It was a huge amount, so much so that he had to "lay it on her."

Think of what this told her, every step of the way home. Like anyone, Ruth must have had moments of doubt, moments when she wondered if Boaz would get cold feet and change his mind, moments when she wondered whether or not he really meant all of those words of love he spoke to her.

But every one of those doubts would have been short lived, since with every step she took she could literally feel the weight of his love pressing down on her shoulders in the form of all of that grain. Her thoughts would then turn from doubt to "Boaz really means it when he says he loves me. Boaz really is going to try everything in his power to have me! If he is willing to send me home with this much, he is very serious about me."

Think of this in terms of the picture it draws for us of the relationship between us and Christ, our Kinsman Redeemer. Are there moments when you doubt His affection for you and His intentions toward you? Pray tell, what is the weight of all the goodness that He has laid on your shoulders? Can we really doubt His affection while nearly bowed down under the weight of His day-by-day goodness?

A searching question

Ruth 3:16 *And when she came to her mother in law, she said,* **Who art thou, my daughter?** *And she told her all that the man had done to her.*

Ruth was coming home, alone, and that is not what Naomi expected. Remember, not only did Ruth not know about the other relative, Naomi was unaware of him as well. Naomi fully expected to *not* see Ruth coming home that day. She expected Boaz to wed her and take her to his home at once! So, when she saw Ruth coming back, she was utterly perplexed.

We then see Naomi asking about Ruth's identity. How long had she known her?

Understand, Naomi knew who Ruth *had been,* she was asking who she was *now...*

Ruth, are you who you have always been, a widow, a gleaner, a girl that has no one to claim as family other than an old mother-in-law?

Are you still her, or are you Ruth, the girl who is about to walk down the aisle?

You asked him to marry you, Ruth, so has your identity changed? Who are you?

Ruth then unfolded for Naomi all that had transpired. I imagine aged Naomi sucked in her breath in horror when she heard of the other kinsman. How could she have been so foolish as to miss not one but two living relatives, two possible kinsman redeemers?

A satisfied acknowledgment

Ruth 3:17 *And she said, These six measures of barley gave he me; for he said to me, Go not empty unto thy mother in law.*

In this verse we are given a bit of a window into the heart of Boaz, and peering into it, we find an enjoyable thing: a sense of humor. In sending what he sent and saying what he said, we may understand his message this way: "I know that your mother-in-law has been the one behind the scenes pulling all of the strings on this for the last couple of months… tell her I said, 'Thanks, Naomi, job well done.'"

A stirred-up man

Ruth 3:18 *Then said she, Sit still, my daughter, until thou know how the matter will fall: for the man will not be in rest, until he have finished the thing this day.*

When Boaz spoke to Ruth in the middle of the night, he told her he would handle this "in the morning." Not later in the day, not sometime during the week, but in the morning.

Boaz was stirred up over Ruth.

Jesus, our Kinsman Redeemer, is stirred up over us. Rejoice, Gentile bride; your Boaz/Jesus is in love with you!

Chapter 13
Mr. "Hey, You There!"

Ruth 4:1 *Then went Boaz up to the gate, and sat him down there: and, behold, the kinsman of whom Boaz spake came by; unto whom he said, Ho, such a one! turn aside, sit down here. And he turned aside, and sat down. 2 And he took ten men of the elders of the city, and said, Sit ye down here. And they sat down. 3 And he said unto the kinsman, Naomi, that is come again out of the country of Moab, selleth a parcel of land, which was our brother Elimelech's: 4 And I thought to advertise thee, saying, Buy it before the inhabitants, and before the elders of my people. If thou wilt redeem it, redeem it: but if thou wilt not redeem it, then tell me, that I may know: for there is none to redeem it beside thee; and I am after thee. And he said, I will redeem it. 5 Then said Boaz, What day thou buyest the field of the hand of Naomi, thou must buy it also of Ruth the Moabitess, the wife of the dead, to raise up the name of the dead upon his inheritance. 6 And the kinsman said, I cannot redeem it for myself, lest I mar mine own inheritance: redeem thou my right to thyself; for I cannot redeem it.*

Naomi told Ruth, "Just sit right here. That man will not be in rest until he finishes the thing this very day."

And that brings us to our text for this chapter.

A unique greeting

Ruth 4:1 *Then went Boaz up to the gate, and sat him down there: and, behold, the kinsman of whom Boaz spake came by; unto whom he said, Ho, such a one! turn aside, sit down here. And he turned aside, and sat down.* **2** *And he took ten men of the elders of the city, and said, Sit ye down here. And they sat down.*

If you are not familiar with the city gates of ancient towns, you may quickly come to the wrong conclusion when you see something like this. The text tells us that Boaz went up to the gate and sat down there.

This was not a case of a man wandering out into the pasture to the fence and propping up alongside the gate. The gates of a city in the ancient world was where the business of the city and of the city government took place. This was specifically stated back in the wilderness wanderings and the time of Moses:

Deuteronomy 16:18 *Judges and officers shalt thou make thee in all thy gates, which the LORD thy God giveth thee, throughout thy tribes: and they shall judge the people with just judgment.*

We see an actual example of it in history from more than four hundred years before that:

Genesis 19:1 *And there came two angels to Sodom at even; and Lot sat in the gate of Sodom: and Lot seeing them rose up to meet them; and he bowed himself with his face toward the ground;*

Genesis 19:9 *And they said, Stand back. And they said again, This one fellow came in to sojourn, and he will needs be a judge: now will we deal worse with thee, than with them. And they pressed sore upon the man, even Lot, and came near to break the door.*

Lot sat in the gate of Sodom, and that is why verse nine shows the men of Sodom sarcastically referring to him being a judge.

The city gates were normally two-story arrangements with an inner gate and an outer gate, and the

130

business of the city was conducted within that enclosure. Sometimes in smaller towns, as commentator Adam Clarke has noted, it was just "a roofed building, unenclosed by walls." That was almost certainly the case in Bethlehem.

So when Boaz went to the gate of the city that morning, he was going on legal business.

Boaz went up to that gate and sat down. The next thing we read is that "behold, the kinsman of whom Boaz spake came by." We do not know if it was simply his regular business that consistently brought him there, or if he was there just by the providence of God at that moment. One way or the other, Boaz somehow ended up right where he needed to be to speak to exactly who he needed to speak to. And it is at that point that one of the most hilarious things you will ever see takes place:

Ruth 4:1 *Then went Boaz up to the gate, and sat him down there: and, behold, the kinsman of whom Boaz spake came by; unto whom he said, **Ho, such a one!** turn aside, sit down here. And he turned aside, and sat down.*

Ho, such a one. What in the world is that about?

Perhaps there is some deep Hebrew meaning behind it. Let us hear from Adam Clarke one more time as to what this means:

"Mr. Such-a-one of such a place."

Ho, such a one. Mr. Such-a-one of such a place. May I be very plain and tell you what this means?

"Hey! You there!"

That, friends, is exactly what this means. Boaz got to the gate, sat down, and waited for someone that he knew very well to come by. This man was not some random stranger; he was family. In fact, as we will see in a moment, other than Naomi this was the only family he had left on earth. In other words, Boaz knew this man.

And yet, he refers to him as Mr. "Hey! You there!"

Have you ever been outwardly composed, but inwardly so excited or jumbled that when you tried to speak your mind just sort of drew a blank? I cannot think of any other explanation for what just happened here.

This is truly a unique greeting.

Well, Boaz got Mr. Hey! You There's attention. And when he did, he called him over to sit down. Then he called in a few others to sit down as well:

Ruth 4:2 *And he took ten men of the elders of the city, and said, Sit ye down here. And they sat down.*

When Boaz got those ten elders seated, their version of court was literally then in session. It was a much simpler and more logical time when things could be settled this quickly and this easily.

An unusual opportunity

Ruth 4:3 *And he said unto the kinsman, Naomi, that is come again out of the country of Moab, selleth a parcel of land, which was our brother Elimelech's: **4** And I thought to advertise thee, saying, Buy it before the inhabitants, and before the elders of my people. If thou wilt redeem it, redeem it: but if thou wilt not redeem it, then tell me, that I may know: for there is none to redeem it beside thee; and I am after thee. And he said, I will redeem it.*

We do not really tend to think of land the way that the Jews thought of it. Most all of us have simply gone somewhere that we like and bought something that we liked. But with the Jews, their land was given to them as an inheritance by God.

You see, hundreds of years before, God had promised Abraham and his descendants the land. But it was not long after that that they ended up as slaves down in Egypt. For four hundred years their God-given inheritance was in the possession of others.

But there came a day when God changed all of that. God sent the people a deliverer named Moses. After a short trip that ended up taking forty years, they finally received that land.

But not without a fight. Joshua, successor to Moses, had to lead the people through years of war to claim the promised land. The land was then divided amongst the tribes, and everyone remembered how serious of a command God had given in regard to them maintaining possession of it:

Leviticus 25:23 *The land shall not be sold for ever: for the land is mine; for ye are strangers and sojourners with me.*

And yet there was a case in which the land could be sold. It was actually mentioned two verses after that prohibition that we just read:

Leviticus 25:25 *If thy brother be waxen poor, and hath sold away some of his possession, and if any of his kin come to redeem it, then shall he redeem that which his brother sold.*

It is still talking about the land when it refers to some of his possession. If you continue reading all that the law said about the land, in cases of poverty the land could be sold, but only to another Jewish person. It was Jewish land, Jewish inheritance, and was never to be sold outside of the nation of Israel. And within the nation of Israel, it could only be sold in cases of poverty.

This was the case that Boaz was presenting to Mr. Hey You. He was pointing out that Naomi, due to her widowhood and the ravages of the famine, was poverty-stricken and was thus selling a piece of land. As the next of kin, Mr. Hey You had the right to buy it.

This was an unusual opportunity. We buy and sell land every day in our country. They did not. Again, the land was an inheritance to them. They may sell everything else, but they were only going to sell the land in cases of great hardship.

If you were a realtor in those days, you were going to be sitting around twiddling your thumbs a lot, because there simply was not much selling of land at all.

Boaz knew this. Mr. Hey You knew this. And Mr. Hey You was only all too excited and willing to buy the land:

"And he said, I will redeem it."

That word for redeem is the exact same word we have seen earlier, the word for the kinsman redeemer. Mr. Hey You was perfectly willing to be a kinsman redeemer…to a piece of land. He was more than willing to "rescue" a piece of land.

But Boaz was playing a very shrewd game, and the other shoe was about to drop.

An uncaring conclusion

Ruth 4:5 *Then said Boaz, What day thou buyest the field of the hand of Naomi, thou must buy it also of Ruth the Moabitess, the wife of the dead, to raise up the name of the dead upon his inheritance.*

When Boaz began speaking to Mr. Hey You, he only mentioned the land. Mr. Hey You was all too excited to buy that. That is as predictable as the rising of the sun.

But then Boaz dropped the other shoe. There was not just a land purchase involved in the deal. There was also a woman who would have to be married. One could not simply pick and choose what parts of the role of the kinsman redeemer he wanted to fulfill. It was all or nothing. Whoever bought the land also had to take the wife that came with it, in this case, Ruth. Ruth the Moabitess.

And suddenly, Mr. Hey You, who was all excited about buying the land, changed his tune:

Ruth 4:6 *And the kinsman said, I cannot redeem it for myself, lest I mar mine own inheritance: redeem thou my right to thyself; for I cannot redeem it.*

There is really no way to overstate the cutting words that this man just spoke. By taking Ruth to him, he would be "marring his inheritance." That is from the Hebrew word *shacath*, and it means to ruin, corrupt, pervert, destroy, rot, and decay.

The man was practically puking on the ground as he spoke words of refusal about this (in his mind) awful, dirty, pagan, low-life foreigner.

Now let's look at this from two angles. From Boaz's side of the fence, this was glorious. Boaz could not possibly have cared less about the land. Boaz was not there because he loved a piece of ground; he was there because he loved Ruth.

Boaz did not drop handfuls of purpose to a piece of ground; he dropped handfuls of purpose to a woman. Boaz did not speak of how well regarded a piece of ground was; he spoke of how well regarded a woman was. Boaz did not reach parched corn to a piece of ground; he reached parched corn to a woman. Boaz did not agree to spread his skirt over a piece of ground; he agreed to spread his skirt over a woman. Boaz did not tell his young men not to touch a piece of ground; he told them not to touch a woman. For Boaz, this was about Ruth, all about Ruth, only about Ruth.

But what in the world is up with this other guy, Mr. Hey You? Why in the world is he so different from Boaz? Why was Boaz so tenderhearted toward a Moabitess, and this guy so hardhearted toward a Moabitess?

When you learn the answer to that, it may well change your view of the entire book of Ruth, and it will definitely elevate your hopefully high estimation of the goodness and graciousness of God.

The answer to the question we are asking about Ruth chapter four is actually found in Ruth chapter one.

Ruth 1:1 *Now it came to pass in the days when the judges ruled, that there was a famine in the land. And a certain man of Bethlehemjudah went to sojourn in the country of Moab, he, and his wife, and his two sons. 2 And the name of the man was Elimelech, and the name of his wife Naomi, and the name of his two sons Mahlon and Chilion, Ephrathites of Bethlehemjudah. And they came into the country of Moab, and continued there. 3 And Elimelech Naomi's husband died; and she was left, and her two sons. 4 And they took them wives of the women of Moab; the name of the one was Orpah, and the name of the other Ruth: and they dwelled there about ten years. 5 And Mahlon and Chilion died also both of them; and the woman was left of* *her two sons and her husband.* **6** *Then she arose with her daughters in law, that she might return from the country of Moab: for she had heard in the country of Moab how that the LORD had visited his people in giving them bread.* **7** *Wherefore she went forth out of the place where she was, and her two daughters in law with her; and they went on the way to return unto the land of Judah.* **8** *And Naomi said unto her two daughters in law, Go, return each to her mother's house: the LORD deal kindly with you, as ye have dealt with the dead, and with me.* **9** *The LORD grant you that ye may find rest, each of you in the house of her husband. Then she kissed them; and they lifted up their voice, and wept.* **10** *And they said unto her, Surely we will return with thee unto thy people.* **11** *And Naomi said, Turn again, my daughters: why will ye go with me? are there yet any more sons in my womb, that they may be your husbands?* **12** *Turn again, my daughters, go your way; for I am too old to have an husband. If I should say, I have hope, if I should have an husband also to night, and should also bear sons;* **13** *Would ye tarry for them till they were grown? would ye stay for them from having husbands? nay, my daughters; for it grieveth me much for your sakes that the hand of the LORD is gone out against me.* **14** *And they lifted up their voice, and wept again: and Orpah kissed her mother in law; but Ruth clave unto her.*

Years ago, someone wrote a Christmas song called "Do You See What I See?"

In this passage, that is my question. Do you see what I see?

There was an exact number of young, marriageable widows who needed a husband, a kinsman redeemer. That number was "two."

Over in Bethlehem, just across the river, there was an exact number of potential kinsman redeemers available. That number was "two."

Two women who needed husbands, two men available to be husbands. Two men who, under normal circumstances would never have anything to do with a Moabite girl.

One of those girls, Orpah, knew that she ought to go to God's country. But she looked that direction, could not see any possible way for things to work out, and so she remained in her pagan land worshiping at the feet of her false god.

The other of those girls, Ruth, knew that she ought to go to God's country. She looked that direction, could not see any possible way for things to work out, and yet chose to forsake her pagan land and trust God anyway.

One walked by sight; the other walked by faith.

When Ruth got to Bethlehem, God brought her across the path of Boaz. Everything that happened from that moment forward softened Boaz' heart and made him change his views on the subject.

Why was Mr. Hey You so cold toward Ruth? Because Ruth was not for him; Orpah was. Had Orpah stepped out on faith the way Ruth did, the same God who softened Boaz's heart could have and doubtless would have done the same thing to the heart of Mr. Hey You.

There was enough for Orpah in God's land.

There will be enough for you as well.

Every child of God will face situations where God does not tell us all of the details. He so prizes faith that from time to time He will put us into a situation where the only two options we have are to exercise faith or to miss out on the blessings that He has for us.

There was enough for Orpah, but she missed it.

Don't make that same mistake in your life.

Chapter 14
The Day Boaz Bought a Bride

Ruth 4:7 *Now this was the manner in former time in Israel concerning redeeming and concerning changing, for to confirm all things; a man plucked off his shoe, and gave it to his neighbour: and this was a testimony in Israel.* **8** *Therefore the kinsman said unto Boaz, Buy it for thee. So he drew off his shoe.* **9** *And Boaz said unto the elders, and unto all the people, Ye are witnesses this day, that I have bought all that was Elimelech's, and all that was Chilion's and Mahlon's, of the hand of Naomi.* **10** *Moreover Ruth the Moabitess, the wife of Mahlon, have I purchased to be my wife, to raise up the name of the dead upon his inheritance, that the name of the dead be not cut off from among his brethren, and from the gate of his place: ye are witnesses this day.* **11** *And all the people that were in the gate, and the elders, said, We are witnesses. The LORD make the woman that is come into thine house like Rachel and like Leah, which two did build the house of Israel: and do thou worthily in Ephratah, and be famous in Bethlehem:* **12** *And let thy house be like the house of Pharez, whom Tamar bare unto Judah, of the seed which the LORD shall give thee of this young woman.*

Boaz wanted Ruth. Mr. Hey You wanted nothing to do with Ruth and rejected her in the harshest terms possible.

And that brings us to our text for this chapter.

139

A barefoot testimony

Ruth 4:7 *Now this was the manner in former time in Israel concerning redeeming and concerning changing, for to confirm all things; a man plucked off his shoe, and* **gave it to his neighbour**: *and this was a testimony in Israel.* **8** *Therefore the kinsman said unto Boaz, Buy it for thee. So he drew off his shoe.*

There is clearly something that takes place in this passage that is foreign to our modern, Western culture. Boaz has offered Ho Such a One the opportunity to buy the land and marry the girl. Ho Such a One, Mr. Hey You, rejected that offer. As he did, he reached down and took his shoe off.

What is that about? Was he about to smack Boaz with it for insulting him by asking if he would like to marry a Moabitess? No, not at all. In fact, this was something that pointed to the shame of the shoeless, not to the shame of Boaz or anyone else.

This was not something that he thought up on the spur of the moment. In fact, it was long established legal practice. In this case, though, there was actually supposed to be another part to it. Let's go back to the law of Moses and let me show you what was happening here.

Deuteronomy 25:7 *And if the man like not to take his brother's wife, then let his brother's wife go up to the gate unto the elders, and say, My husband's brother refuseth to raise up unto his brother a name in Israel, he will not perform the duty of my husband's brother.* **8** *Then the elders of his city shall call him, and speak unto him: and if he stand to it, and say, I like not to take her;* **9** *Then shall his brother's wife come unto him in the presence of the elders, and loose his shoe from off his foot, and spit in his face, and shall answer and say, So shall it be done unto that man that will not build up his brother's house.* **10** *And his name shall be called in Israel, The house of him that hath his shoe loosed.*

The kinsman redeemer had both blessings and responsibilities that came with the role. He was to pay the debts, he was to act as a revenger of blood, he was to buy the land, he was to marry the girl. All of that was a high and holy calling, one that pointed to none other than the coming Messiah Himself.

If a man was not willing to fulfill his role as a kinsman redeemer, he was to be publicly humiliated. He was to give up a shoe, and the woman was allowed to spit in his face.

Forever thereafter he would bear the stigma, he would be called "the house of him that hath his shoe loosed."

Now go back to the book of Ruth with me. What part was left out in this instance? The woman spitting in his face. That did not happen here.

There are conjectures and speculations that just run wild concerning why this was left out. The truth is, any one opinion is probably just as good as another opinion because the Bible text does not actually tell us why this part was left out. That being the case, may I humbly offer my speculation?

Think about the character of Ruth. Think of everything you know about her tender and humble spirit.

Do you think Ruth even had it in her to spit in a man's face, even a man who treated her as harshly as this one? I do not. My speculation is that Boaz did not bring her there that day because he knew good and well Ruth was too sweet and too tender to do that even to someone who had humiliated her.

The second part of the ceremony was fulfilled that day. A man who left home that day with two perfectly good shoes, a man who expected to come home that night with two perfectly good shoes, found himself hobbling away with one bare foot.

Pay careful attention. The text says that this was to "confirm" all things. In other words, this was the legal proof of what had taken place. What I am saying is, the man did not get his shoe back. He left that day with one foot bare, and Boaz left that day carrying a guy's shoe in his hand. As

Mr. Hey You walked away that day, it was with a missing footwear induced limp.

This is not something he was expecting when he got up that morning…him walking away missing the shoe was a barefoot testimony to the fact that he had passed up an opportunity and neglected a responsibility.

A bold purchase

Ruth 4:9 *And Boaz said unto the elders, and unto all the people, Ye are witnesses this day, that I have bought all that was Elimelech's, and all that was Chilion's and Mahlon's, of the hand of Naomi.* **10** *Moreover Ruth the Moabitess, the wife of Mahlon, have I purchased to be my wife, to raise up the name of the dead upon his inheritance, that the name of the dead be not cut off from among his brethren, and from the gate of his place: ye are witnesses this day.*

Look at the scene at the gate at that moment.

There is a guy walking away missing a shoe.

There are the elders that Boaz called the witnesses, but there is also a huge crowd that has gathered, referred to as "all the people."

Mr. Hey You was embarrassed at the very thought of taking Ruth to be his wife. But here is Boaz taking Ruth to be his wife, not quietly, not like he is embarrassed, but as thrilled as a child on Christmas morning who has just gotten every single item on his wish list.

Boaz is shouting boldly for everyone to hear, "I have taken Ruth, the Moabitess, to be my wife! Everybody keep your eyes to yourself and don't even think about trying to get her because she is mine, she is mine, she is mine!"

Notice that in verse nine the very first words out of his mouth were, "you are witnesses." Then notice that in verse ten he says the exact same thing again.

Boaz wanted to make really, really, really sure that everyone knew Ruth was his. He was not the least bit shy about it or embarrassed over it, this was the happiest day of his life, taking this little former pagan, Gentile bride to be his wife.

A beautiful omission

Ruth 4:11 *And all the people that were in the gate, and the elders, said, We are witnesses. The LORD make the woman that is come into thine house like Rachel and like Leah, which two did build the house of Israel: and do thou worthily in Ephratah, and be famous in Bethlehem:* **12** *And let thy house be like the house of Pharez, whom Tamar bare unto Judah, of the seed which the LORD shall give thee of this young woman.*

A few minutes earlier Mr. Hey You had been confronted with an opportunity to buy a piece of land, and he was thrilled at the opportunity.

And then he was informed that he would have to marry Ruth as part of the package deal as a kinsman redeemer. Suddenly, that land was not so attractive to him anymore.

He hobbled away, really regretting that he was not able to secure that piece of property for himself.

But then Boaz begins to speak. And when he does, at no time does he ever specifically mention that land. And when the elders speak here in verses eleven and twelve, they pick up on that immediately:

Ruth 4:11 *And all the people that were in the gate, and the elders, said, We are witnesses. The LORD make the woman that is come into thine house like Rachel and like Leah, which two did build the house of Israel: and do thou worthily in Ephratah, and be famous in Bethlehem:* **12** *And let thy house be like the house of Pharez, whom Tamar bare unto Judah, of the seed which the LORD shall give thee of this young woman.*

Why did these witnesses to a legal proceeding in which land changed hands not even mention the land in any way shape or form? Because it was very clear to them that Boaz could not have cared less about the land; all Boaz wanted was the girl. The land was omitted in their opening legal statement to him because they knew that the land was irrelevant to him.

A blessed inclusion

Ruth 4:12 *And let thy house be like the house of Pharez, whom Tamar bare unto Judah, of the seed which the LORD shall give thee of this young woman.*

Verse twelve is an incredibly significant verse that usually gets almost entirely overlooked in all of this. Please remember that the words of verse twelve are being spoken out loud, in public, to all of the crowd gathered around. These words are being spoken by the elders, the legal witnesses to all that has taken place.

The setting of verse twelve begins back with what they said in verse eleven, so let's look at that one more time.

Ruth 4:11 *And all the people that were in the gate, and the elders, said, We are witnesses. The LORD make the woman that is come into thine house like **Rachel** and like **Leah**, which two did build the house of Israel: and do thou worthily in Ephratah, and be famous in Bethlehem:*

When these elders spoke of Ruth, they spoke out loud of who they hoped the Lord would make her to be like. They mentioned the names of two very famous people in Israel, Rachel and Leah.

Rachel and Leah were very respectable to them. They were legends. They were the mothers of the tribes of the nation of Israel.

All of the crowd standing around is hearing this, and they know that it is being applied to Ruth, Ruth the Moabitess.

What must they be thinking?

Sure, a Moabitess will be like Rachel and Leah... when pigs fly.

Then these elders, God bless their wise hearts, I am guessing that maybe they saw the reactions on those faces, because what they said next was completely unexpected:

144

Ruth 4:12 *And let thy house be like the house of Pharez, whom Tamar bare unto Judah, of the seed which the LORD shall give thee of this young woman.*

Pharez? Tamar? Those are not names that will be immediately recognizable to a person who spends little time in Scripture. Rachel and Leah, yes. Even a great many lost people could give you the life's story of those two. But Pharez and Tamar? Who are they, and what are these elders driving at?

Look at their account, and you will figure it out pretty quickly.

Genesis 38:6 *And Judah took a wife for Er his firstborn, whose name was Tamar. 7 And Er, Judah's firstborn, was wicked in the sight of the LORD; and the LORD slew him. 8 And Judah said unto Onan, Go in unto thy brother's wife, and marry her, and raise up seed to thy brother. 9 And Onan knew that the seed should not be his; and it came to pass, when he went in unto his brother's wife, that he spilled it on the ground, lest that he should give seed to his brother. 10 And the thing which he did displeased the LORD: wherefore he slew him also. 11 Then said Judah to Tamar his daughter in law, Remain a widow at thy father's house, till Shelah my son be grown: for he said, Lest peradventure he die also, as his brethren did. And Tamar went and dwelt in her father's house. 12 And in process of time the daughter of Shuah Judah's wife died; and Judah was comforted, and went up unto his sheepshearers to Timnath, he and his friend Hirah the Adullamite. 13 And it was told Tamar, saying, Behold thy father in law goeth up to Timnath to shear his sheep. 14 And she put her widow's garments off from her, and covered her with a vail, and wrapped herself, and sat in an open place, which is by the way to Timnath; for she saw that Shelah was grown, and she was not given unto him to wife. 15 When Judah saw her, he thought her to be an harlot; because she had covered her face. 16 And he turned unto her by the way, and said, Go to, I pray thee, let me come in unto thee; (for he knew not that she was his daughter in law.) And she said, What wilt thou* *give me, that thou mayest come in unto me? 17 And he said, I will send thee a kid from the flock. And she said, Wilt thou give me a pledge, till thou send it? 18 And he said, What pledge shall I give thee? And she said, Thy signet, and thy bracelets, and thy staff that is in thine hand. And he gave it her, and came in unto her, and she conceived by him. 19 And she arose, and went away, and laid by her vail from her, and put on the garments of her widowhood. 20 And Judah sent the kid by the hand of his friend the Adullamite, to receive his pledge from the woman's hand: but he found her not. 21 Then he asked the men of that place, saying, Where is the harlot, that was openly by the way side? And they said, There was no harlot in this place. 22 And he returned to Judah, and said, I cannot find her; and also the men of the place said, that there was no harlot in this place. 23 And Judah said, Let her take it to her, lest we be shamed: behold, I sent this kid, and thou hast not found her. 24 And it came to pass about three months after, that it was told Judah, saying, Tamar thy daughter in law hath played the harlot; and also, behold, she is with child by whoredom. And Judah said, Bring her forth, and let her be burnt. 25 When she was brought forth, she sent to her father in law, saying, By the man, whose these are, am I with child: and she said, Discern, I pray thee, whose are these, the signet, and bracelets, and staff. 26 And Judah acknowledged them, and said, She hath been more righteous than I; because that I gave her not to Shelah my son. And he knew her again no more. 27 And it came to pass in the time of her travail, that, behold, twins were in her womb. 28 And it came to pass, when she travailed, that the one put out his hand: and the midwife took and bound upon his hand a scarlet thread, saying, This came out first. 29 And it came to pass, as he drew back his hand, that, behold, his brother came out: and she said, How hast thou broken forth? this breach be upon thee: therefore his name was called Pharez. 30 And afterward came out his brother, that had the scarlet thread upon his hand: and his name was called Zarah.*

It is readily apparent that, while Rachel and Leah were looked upon as legends, Tamar was certainly not. Tamar, reacting to the lies and sins of her father-in-law, committed an unspeakable sin of her own. And the product of that sin was a son, a son named Pharez.

And yet, from that bad beginning, the Lord did great things through the seed of Tamar. In fact, when these elders mentioned Pharez and Tamar to those very likely skeptical hearers standing around, those names could not fail but to ring a bell in their heads. You see, the descendants of Pharez became the inhabitants of Bethlehem, including the family of Elimilech... (Clark, 2:202)

These elders were basically saying to everyone who would listen, "Yes, Ruth was a Moabitess. But she has come to trust under the wings of the God of Israel; she is not what she once was. We believe God can and will do something great through this Gentile bride who has been purchased by a Jewish kinsman redeemer."

They were saying, "Don't write her off just because her past was bad. All of us have a past, but all of us including her have a future too. Boaz thinks so much of this woman that he has bought her when someone else rejected her; you just wait, God is going to do great things with this woman."

Every bit of that is a perfect picture of Christ our Kinsman Redeemer purchasing us to Himself.

Every bit of that is a perfect picture of the fact that God desires to do great things through us, no matter what our past may be.

Ruth went on to become the great-grandmother of David the king, and Christ Himself came directly through her bloodline.

What could you be for Christ?

One last thing. We know absolutely nothing about the house, the physical dwelling place of Ruth and Boaz. But do you realize that we do know one thing that was in the house from that point on?

A shoe.

From that day forward, there was a single shoe in that house, sitting there as a silent testimony to the day that Boaz bought a bride.

I can just imagine Ruth wandering through that house on some days when she was feeling dark and depressed for some reason, maybe circumstances not going so well in her life, and then she would pass by and glance over in the corner and see that shoe...

I can just imagine her saying, "I'm his! I'm his! I'm his! It's going to be okay; I'm his!"

Chapter 15
From Barren to Blessed by Way of Brokenness

Ruth 4:13 *So Boaz took Ruth, and she was his wife: and when he went in unto her, the LORD gave her conception, and she bare a son.* **14** *And the women said unto Naomi, Blessed be the LORD, which hath not left thee this day without a kinsman, that his name may be famous in Israel.* **15** *And he shall be unto thee a restorer of thy life, and a nourisher of thine old age: for thy daughter in law, which loveth thee, which is better to thee than seven sons, hath born him.* **16** *And Naomi took the child, and laid it in her bosom, and became nurse unto it.* **17** *And the women her neighbours gave it a name, saying, There is a son born to Naomi; and they called his name Obed: he is the father of Jesse, the father of David.* **18** *Now these are the generations of Pharez: Pharez begat Hezron,* **19** *And Hezron begat Ram, and Ram begat Amminadab,* **20** *And Amminadab begat Nahshon, and Nahshon begat Salmon,* **21** *And Salmon begat Boaz, and Boaz begat Obed,* **22** *And Obed begat Jesse, and Jesse begat David.*

Let's look at verse thirteen once more as we begin, and then I am going to come right back to it at the end of the chapter.

Ruth 4:13 *So Boaz took Ruth, and she was his wife: and when he went in unto her, the LORD gave her conception, and she bare a son.*

Ruth had a son. Ruth became a mother. The rest of this passage will say a great deal about the child and about all that came from that child.

A new lease on life for Naomi

Ruth 4:13 *So Boaz took Ruth, and she was his wife: and when he went in unto her, the LORD gave her conception, and she bare a son.* **14** *And the women said unto Naomi, Blessed be the LORD, which hath not left thee this day without a kinsman, that his name may be famous in Israel.* **15** *And he shall be unto thee a restorer of thy life, and a nourisher of thine old age: for thy daughter in law, which loveth thee, which is better to thee than seven sons, hath born him.* **16** *And Naomi took the child, and laid it in her bosom, and became nurse unto it.*

Ruth went through labor, Ruth bore a child, yet Naomi was the one the women started talking to. Ruth doing right did not just benefit her: it became a new lease on life for Naomi. Naomi thought she had nothing, and thanks to Ruth ended up with everything.

If you really care about people, do right, every single day.

A name to fit a family

Ruth 4:17 *And the women her neighbours gave it a name, saying, There is a son born to Naomi; and they called his name Obed: he is the father of Jesse, the father of David.*

Obed. It means "servant." Why that name? What had he ever done? Nothing, yet. But what was his family like? Think of Boaz working beside his employees. Think of Ruth gleaning after the reapers for the benefit of her aged mother-in-law. This child was given his name because of his family's reputation.

The best inheritance you can give your kids is a good, godly name to live up to.

A never-ending supply of grace

Ruth 4:18 *Now these are the generations of Pharez: Pharez begat Hezron,* **19** *And Hezron begat Ram, and Ram begat Amminadab,* **20** *And Amminadab begat Nahshon, and Nahshon begat Salmon,* **21** *And Salmon begat Boaz, and Boaz begat Obed,* **22** *And Obed begat Jesse, and Jesse begat David.*

Who was Pharez? The illegitimate child of an incestuous relationship.

Who was Salmon? The guy who married a former prostitute.

Who was Boaz? the guy who married a former pagan.

In case you were wondering, God isn't looking for people who are so good that He can take them and show them off, "Look how pretty and shiny they are!" God is looking for people to help show off His grace. That is good news indeed. Not many of us qualify as "pretty and shiny," but every one of us wretched sinners certainly qualify as potential recipients of grace!

A narrow pathway that led to joy

Go back to verse thirteen one more time:

Ruth 4:13 *So Boaz took Ruth, and she was his wife: and when he went in unto her,* **the LORD gave her conception**, *and she bare a son.*

It is not always said this way in Scripture. In fact, this is the only time it is ever said this way!

In other words, God was trying to grab our attention.

By the time people get to the end of the book of Ruth, the one direction they are normally not looking is back. But it is here above all, this last part of Ruth, that we ought to take a moment and look back. In fact, if we do not, we really will miss the entire point of the book.

151

Go back to the very beginning of the story...

A girl named Ruth was going about her daily life there in Moab. And then one day a new family moved into town. There were two boys in the family, one of them was named Mahlon. Somewhere along the line Mahlon and Ruth caught each other's eye. That led to a wedding as Ruth started a new life full of expectations.

One of those expectations was that she would have children; she would become a mother.

During the first year of their marriage, that did not happen. Nor did it happen on the second year or the third or the fourth...

Ten years. Ruth was married for ten years and never could have a child. She was barren. There was no greater shame, no greater heartbreak that a woman in those days and culture could be going through.

And then one day things got even worse; her husband Mahlon died. Now she was not only barren; she was also a widow.

Her life was in shambles.

Then she began a journey. Her mother-in-law, Naomi, had determined to go back home to Bethlehem. At first, both Ruth and her sister-in-law, Orpah, proclaimed that they would absolutely go with her. But when all of the details were laid out, Orpah went back home, and Ruth, barren Ruth, alone went with Naomi.

And that journey ended up with her married, with a son. Ruth went from barren to blessed by way of brokenness. The fact that she had a child with Boaz but not with Mahlon pretty clearly indicates that he was the problem, not her. And yet the only thing that changed that paradigm was for her to be broken into bits.

Not being broken is not an option in anyone's life, at all. We are a fallen people living in a fallen, cursed world. So, I say again, not being broken is an option that is not even on the table, for anyone.

152

But a very good God knows just what to do about that. The devil wants our brokenness to be a "dead end." He nails up a sign at the end of our brokenness avenue.

But for those willing to keep following God, He kicks the sign down and turns the dead end into a pathway.

Psalm 113:7 *He raiseth up the poor out of the dust, and lifteth the needy out of the dunghill;* **8** *That he may set him with princes, even with the princes of his people.*

Ruth was an uncut gem, just waiting to be discovered. So was Boaz. They were diamonds in the darkness, jewels of rarest worth, gems that the God of heaven refused to allow to stay hidden and unpolished.

What might you be in God's hands?

I suppose that will depend on whether you go Ruth's way or Orpah's way, Boaz' way or the way of Mr. Hey You.

Choose wisely.

Works Cited

Clarke, Adam, *Clarke's Commentary.* Abingdon-Cokesbury Press, 6 vols.

Henry, Matthew. *Matthew Henry's Commentary on the Whole Bible.* Vol 2, Revell.

Newell, http://www.historylink.org/File/5235

Patrick, Lowth, Whitby, Lowman Commentary, Power Bible 5.9, Online Publishing, editor Phil Lindner, Bronson, MI, 2010

Other Books by Dr. Bo Wagner

From Footers to Finish Nails
Beyond the Colored Coat
Marriage Makers/Marriage Breakers
Daniel: Breathtaking
Esther: Five Feast and the Finger Prints of God
Nehemiah: A Labor of Love
Romans: Salvation From A-Z
Ruth: Diamonds in the Darkness
Don't Muzzle the Ox
I'm Saved! Now What???

Fiction Titles

The Night Heroes Series:
Cry From the Coal Mine (Vol. 1)
Free Fall (Vol. 2)
Broken Brotherhood (Vol. 3)
The Blade of Black Crow (Vol. 4)
Ghost Ship (Vol. 5)
When Serpents Rise (Vol. 6)
Moth Man (Vol. 7)

Sci-Fi

Zak Blue and the Great Space Chase:
Falcon Wing (Vol. 1)

www.ingramcontent.com/pod-product-compliance
Lightning Source LLC
Chambersburg PA
CBHW072012040426
42447CB00009B/1606